Phebe A. (Phebe Ann) Hanaford

**From Shore to Shore**

And Other Poems

Phebe A. (Phebe Ann) Hanaford

**From Shore to Shore**
*And Other Poems*

ISBN/EAN: 9783744665599

Printed in Europe, USA, Canada, Australia, Japan

Cover: Foto ©Thomas Meinert / pixelio.de

More available books at **www.hansebooks.com**

# FROM SHORE TO SHORE,

## And Other Poems.

BY

PHEBE A. HANAFORD.

"I WILL sing you a song of that beautiful land,
    The far-away home of the soul;
Where no storms ever beat on the glittering strand,
    While the years of eternity roll."

BOSTON:
PUBLISHED BY B. B. RUSSELL, 55 CORNHILL.
SAN FRANCISCO: A. L. BANCROFT & CO.
1871.

Entered, according to Act of Congress, in the year 1870,
By PHEBE A. HANAFORD.
In the Office of the Librarian of Congress, at Washington.

*Boston :*
*Rand, Avery, & Frye, Stereotypers and Printers.*

### Dedicatory Sonnet.

## TO ELLEN E. MILES.

FRIEND of my later years, whose tender love
   Has filled my home with blossoms, sweet though late,
Whose noble heart my spirit must approve,
   As Duty's path thou tread'st with willing feet :
Thy welcome service, at Love's bidding mine,
   As these my rhythmic waifs are gathered now,
Calls for a grateful tribute, and I twine
   This simple wreath, dear NELLIE, for thy brow.
Soul-sister ! may the waiting years for thee
   Pour out a largess of such holy joy
That earth shall seem the porch of heaven to be,
   And songs of praise thy tuneful lips employ !
Then, while eternal years shall onward roll,
Still may we share Love's summer of the soul !

# PREFACE.

THESE poems are offered only to those, who, through love, will not "view them with a critic's eye." They have not been wrought with patient labor, neither have they been quarried from mines of thought, but have sprung spontaneously from seeds which sympathy planted. The manifold cares of a city parish forbid much pruning or trimming; and hence they are given to the public in much the same form as when they first appeared in the various newspapers and magazines whose "poet's corner" they helped to fill. If they may only, in their present dress, gratify the many friends who have asked for them, and in some way bless humanity, and thus glorify God, the writer will be satisfied.

P. A. H.

19 HOME PLACE, NEW HAVEN, CONN.

# CONTENTS.

### POEMS OF CHRISTIAN FAITH.

From Shore to Shore . . . . . . .
Our Home Beyond the Tide . . . . . .
Mankind Moves Onward . . . . . . .
At Evening Time it shall be Light . . . . .
Farther On . . . . . . . . .
Your Heavenly Father knoweth . . . . .
The Day-Star in my Heart . . . . . .
The Eden Above . . . . . . . .
Christ's Invitation . . . . . . . .
That Better Land . . . . . . . .
Verbum Consolationis . . . . . . .
The Coming of Death . . . . . . .
Death and Victory . . . . . . . .
Free Thought . . . . . . . . .
Light in Darkness . . . . . . . .
The Still Hour . . . . . . . . .
God is Love . . . . . . . . .
The Last Supper . . . . . . . .
O River of God, Roll On! . . . . . .
Rejoice Evermore . . . . . . . .
A Vision by Faith . . . . . . . .
A Morning without Clouds . . . . . .

## CONTENTS.

|  | PAGE. |
|---|---|
| Light and Liberty | 57 |
| No more Tears | 58 |
| The Feast of Life | 59 |
| Nearer | 61 |
| Joys to Come | 62 |
| We shall be like Him | 63 |
| The Purpose of Creation | 65 |

### POEMS OF FRIENDSHIP.

| | |
|---|---|
| To "Mabelle" | 69 |
| "Je Vous Remercie" | 72 |
| Birthday Stanzas | 73 |
| Sixtieth Birthday of F. Barden | 74 |
| What shall I wish for Thee | 76 |
| Album Stanzas.— To E. R. | 77 |
| Farewell to Carleton | 78 |
| They say that I Love Thee | 79 |
| Memento Lines to a Friend | 81 |

### SONNETS.

| | |
|---|---|
| William H. Prescott | 85 |
| George Washington | 86 |
| To a Friend in Sadness | 86 |
| Capture of Charleston | 87 |
| A Winter Sonnet | 88 |
| To Joanna Quiner | 88 |
| On seeing a Bust by Miss Quiner | 89 |
| For the Grave of Mrs. A. A. Foster | 90 |
| Liberty *versus* Romanism | 90 |
| Flowers | 91 |

### POEMS OF PATRIOTISM.

| | |
|---|---|
| The Live-Oak Tree | 95 |
| Soldier, Rest! | 97 |

## CONTENTS.

|  | PAGE. |
|---|---|
| The Poet's Prophecy of American Future | 99 |
| Waiting for the Hour | 100 |
| Emancipation | 102 |
| The Patriot's Prayer | 104 |
| The Lawrence Massacre | 106 |
| Where is He? | 107 |
| The Soldier and the Teacher | 109 |
| The Dead Soldier | 112 |
| Jubilee Guns | 113 |
| The Mothers of the Brave | 115 |
| The Destruction of the Merrimac | 116 |
| It is Well! | 118 |
| The Young Soldier | 119 |
| Liberty to All | 120 |
| A Prayer for Abraham Lincoln | 121 |
| The White Hyacinth from Hampton | 123 |
| The Buried Volunteer | 124 |
| A Prayer for the Union | 125 |
| A Flower from a Rebel's Grave | 126 |
| The Siege of Charleston | 128 |
| The Union Army never surrenders | 129 |
| All Quiet Along the Potomac | 131 |
| Freedom in Poland | 132 |

### MEMORIAL POEMS.

|  | |
|---|---|
| The Righteous in Everlasting Remembrance | 137 |
| First Time — Last Time — Next Time | 139 |
| Only Out of Sight | 140 |
| In Memory of Mrs. E. A. Tenney | 142 |
| To A. A. F. | 143 |
| The Ascended Saint | 145 |
| Margaret Fuller | 146 |
| Rev. Arthur Buckminster Fuller | 148 |
| Rev. Dr. Sylvanus Cobb | 150 |

|                              | PAGE. |
|------------------------------|------:|
| Eugene Fuller                | 151   |
| Richard F. Fuller            | 153   |
| The Tree                     | 154   |
| Buried in the Deep           | 155   |
| The Mother of Whittier       | 156   |
| Stephen Grellet              | 157   |
| One Week in Heaven           | 159   |
| Little Josey                 | 161   |
| Live for Others              | 162   |
| Major Soule                  | 163   |
| Elliot's Monument            | 165   |
| My Farewell to 1864          | 166   |

## POEMS OF SYMPATHY.

|                         | PAGE. |
|-------------------------|------:|
| A Baby borne Away       | 171   |
| To a Motherless Friend  | 172   |
| Our Loved One Sleeps    | 174   |
| She is in Heaven        | 175   |
| Kiss me, Mother         | 176   |
| The Answered Prayer     | 178   |
| To a Bereaved Friend    | 180   |
| A Mother in Heaven      | 181   |
| Only and Well Beloved   | 182   |

## MISCELLANEOUS POEMS.

|                              | PAGE. |
|------------------------------|------:|
| No Turning Back              | 187   |
| The Music of the Pines       | 188   |
| The Receding Comet           | 190   |
| My Mother's Voice in Prayer  | 191   |
| To a Daffodil                | 193   |
| The Student's Prayer         | 194   |
| To Maria Mitchell            | 197   |
| Brant Point                  | 198   |

## CONTENTS.

| | PAGE. |
|---|---|
| Dead Hopes | 200 |
| Angelic Language | 202 |
| On the Shore of the Sounding Sea | 203 |
| Violets | 204 |
| The Autumn Rain | 205 |
| Charlotte Brontë Reading the Bible | 207 |
| Death in the State House | 209 |
| The Child's Message | 211 |
| The Children's Concert | 212 |
| Flowers | 214 |
| Niagara | 215 |
| Gospel Consolation | 216 |
| Thoughts after a Snow-Storm | 217 |
| Eagle Rock and Manchester Beach | 219 |
| Eli Ben Israel | 220 |
| The Sorrowful Ten Thousand | 222 |
| The Last Day of Winter | 224 |
| Parting Words | 226 |
| Twilight on Beverly Shore | 227 |
| A Prophecy | 229 |
| Byron | 231 |
| The Palace and the Angel | 232 |
| The Grecian Athlete | 235 |
| The Ride | 236 |
| Christmas Eve | 237 |
| We all do fade as a Leaf | 238 |
| The Book of Job | 240 |
| The Power of the Beautiful | 241 |
| Moonlight on the Ocean | 243 |
| A Tribute of Gratitude | 245 |
| The Boys' Hymn | 246 |
| "Insula Bonæ Fortunæ" | 249 |
| Glory to God Alone | 247 |
| Round Hill | 250 |

## CONTENTS.

| | PAGE. |
|---|---|
| The Love-Feast | 252 |
| Ups and Downs | 253 |
| God Reigns | 254 |
| Return of the Jews to Palestine | 256 |
| The Moonlight Scene | 257 |
| They marry not in Heaven | 259 |
| Rest for the True Laborer | 261 |
| The Shipwreck | 262 |
| Mrs. Hemans on the Sea-Shore | 263 |
| The Midnight Meeting | 264 |
| Wenham-Lake Ice | 264 |
| Rally for Temperance | 266 |
| To One who has sent me the Works of Swedenborg | 267 |
| God and Little Children | 270 |
| Lives written for an Agricultural Fair | 273 |
| The Cross and the Crown | 274 |
| The Question Answered | 275 |

# BIOGRAPHICAL SKETCH.

THE author of these poems is a native of the Island of Nantucket. Her family name was Coffin; and she was born of Quaker parents, May 6, 1829, and on her mother's side is a descendant from Peter Folger, the maternal grandfather of the philosopher and statesman, Benjamin Franklin, and thus related to Lucretia Mott and Maria Mitchell. Until the age of sixteen, she studied in the public and private schools of Nantucket, when she commenced teaching, but still pursued her studies with the late Rev. Ethan Allen, then rector of the Episcopal church on that island. At the early age of thirteen, she commenced writing for the press of her native town. That the child-poet was deeply sensitive to the blight upon our boasted freedom may be seen by the following stanzas, which close a short poem entitled "America," written at the age of thirteen: —

> "Shame, shame the deepest, will be thine,
> Till Freedom's light on all shall shine;
> Till black and white alike are free,
> Blight will forever rest on thee;

> But change the scene, and let the sun
> No injured bondman shine upon,
> Then joy shall reign o'er all the land,
> And high 'midst nations thou shalt stand."

In 1849 she married, and removed to Newton, Mass., where for a year she assisted her husband, Dr. J. H. Hanaford, in teaching, at the same time devoting her leisure hours to literary pursuits. She then returned to Nantucket; and resided there until, in 1857, with her husband and two young children, she removed to the town of Beverly, Mass., where she became personally active in the Temperance cause, since which time she has occupied prominent offices in the Grand and Subordinate lodges of Good Templars. In 1864, she removed to Reading, Mass., where she united with the Universalists of that place, and soon afterwards accepted the editorship of that popular magazine, "The Ladies Repository." Of her success in that direction we need only say, that during her three years' labor there its subscription-list was increased some thousands. In 1866 she commenced preaching in the town of Hingham, Mass., where, in 1868, she was ordained and installed pastor of the First Universalist Church, being the first woman ordained in Massachusetts. Rev. John G. Adams and Rev. Olympia Brown preached the sermons. In 1869 she accepted a call from the Universalist Society at Waltham, and for one year supplied the desk on alternate Sundays at Hingham and Waltham, sending supplies to the vacant pulpit. At the close of the same year, she had a unanimous call from the Universalist church in New Haven, Conn. Precious as were the associations which clustered around her first and dearly-loved parish at Hingham, duty led her to accept the call into a broader field of labor. The following April she took charge of the New-Haven society, and was installed as pastor, June 9, 1870, Rev. Dr. E. H. Chapin preaching the sermon. None but those who know her in her home can conceive of the amount of labor which she performs with her pen. Not only does she write both prose and verse for many of the newspapers and other periodicals of the day, but she has had published ten volumes ; among which is her " Life of Peabody," reaching a sale of sixteen thousand copies; and her " Life of Lincoln," twenty thousand. An edition of five thousand of the latter was published in the German language. She is never idle. Through winter's cold and summer's heat she is still busy with her toil, — active in all the reforms of the day, a prominent worker for woman suffrage, a general favorite in the lecture-field, while as a preacher she is having an enviable success.

E. E. M.

# FROM SHORE TO SHORE.

# FROM SHORE TO SHORE.

IT was a dreamy and delicious day,
  Such as we, blissful, know in later May,
When from the shore a tiny vessel sped,
With hearts as joyous as the skies o'erhead,
Borne with its fairy grace along the wave,
While rippled forth their talk both gay and grave.
The aged sire with snowy locks was there;
The mother also with her brow of care:
Both dear and precious to the youthful band,
Who blend their buoyant hearts with strength of
    hand.
The children gazed afar from out the prow,
And scarce could wait the while their keel should
    plough
Its shining furrow through the yielding tide
To reach the shore upon the other side.
Young love was there to blend the hearts of two:
The maiden smiled; the whispered tale, so new
And yet so old, was still so full of bliss,
They saw no farther shore, nor yet saw this, —
Only each other all the voyage they saw,
Obeying thus the grand, eternal law.
With thoughtful eye, and choosing oft to stand,
Fair Lena's husband views the distant land;

While prattling childhood, at the vessel's side,
Watches the motion of the azure tide.
At last the boatman breaks the silence long,
And begs of youth and maiden each a song.
The maiden coy refuses with a smile;
The youth declares he cannot thus beguile
The hours that float too fast for him away,
Bringing the farewell with the close of day.
Then asks the husband, — proud and glad is he, —
"Dear Lena, sing the song which pleaseth me."
Pleased with his pleasure, sharing Love's reward,
She sings a stanza in Love's sweet accord;
And soft the music floats the waters o'er,
As thus she sings the song, "From Shore to Shore."

> "In childhood's hour with careless joy
>     Upon the stream we glide;
> With youth's bright hopes we gayly speed
>     To reach the other side.
> From shore to shore, from shore to shore,
>     We're gliding on forever:
> Keep watch and ward to guide and guard,
>     O Thou who slumberest never!"

Thus sang the wife; and then, this stanza o'er,
All sang the chorus of this "Shore to Shore."

> "From shore to shore, from shore to shore,
>     We're gliding on forever:
> Keep watch and ward to guide and guard,
>     O Thou who slumberest never!"

Then silence fell, like night on Arab plain,
When ceased the music of that sweet refrain;
And, ere its sweet solemnity was o'er,
They talked together of the far-off shore, —
Not the fair land their mortal eyes descried,
But that so out of sight beyond the tide.
And heart to heart they spoke Faith's earnest word,
Trusting the love revealed by Christ the Lord;
And reverent questions met with answers then,
As silver locks replied to youthful ken;
While young and old rejoiced to know one Eye
Of Love unwearied watched them from the sky.

The noontide came; and on a fairy isle
The party rested for a pleasant while;
And mirth and gladness ruled the fiery hour,
Beneath the shelter of the woodland bower.
And while they rested, at the sire's request,
They sang the songs that tell us of the blest;
And, as they gazed their watery pathway o'er,
Another stanza came, "From Shore to Shore."

"Manhood looks forth with careful glance;
    Time steady plies the oar;
  While old age calmly waits to hear
    The keel upon the shore.
  And when our keel shall grate at last,
    Beyond the rolling river,
  Thy praise we'll sing, while loud shall ring
    The fair, green shore forever."

And then the children there the chorus sang,
While all the woodland with the echoes rang, —

"From shore to shore, from shore to shore,
  We're gliding on forever:
Keep watch and ward to guide and guard,
  O Thou who slumberest never!"

Noon passed: the blazing sun went down the west;
The May-bloom had the isle in beauty drest;
And through its pleasant paths they sauntered long,
Mingling their cheerful talk with shout and song.
The day was rare; all hearts at peace were found;
And love made that sweet isle all hallowed ground.
The aged grandsire, with his silvery crown,
And his companion with her pure renown, —
The village friend, the solace of the poor,
The unwearied watcher by the solemn door, —
They sat, and thought of joys for them in store
When Life should blossom on the other shore;
And, with a peace that faith alone could bring,
They heard their children of that heaven sing,
And blessed the Power which o'er Life's lengthened
    way
Had guided them and guarded, day by day.

When o'er the waters rose the silvery moon,
Their day to lovers ended all too soon,
Once more the boatman called; then gathered they,
And homeward bound once more they launched away.
The grating keel slow glided from the shore,
And they were on the sparkling wave once more.
Homeward they sped with Peace attendant there,
The angel of the hour, serene and fair.
Hope had her pinions folded; for the day
Her promise had fulfilled, and now the way

Was o'er the moonlit tide to home's calm bliss,
The foretaste of the new earth's rest in this.
The lovers' whispered vows were hushed that night,
As hand in hand they watched the shimmering light,
And in the sparkling of their watery way
Beheld the diamonds of their wedding-day
The husband drew his Lena to his side,
And whispered, "Dearer now than when a bride."
The old man looked on all with calm content;
The aged mother, who the day had spent
In large desire that others should be blest,
Now smiled in concert with his thought of rest;
And e'en the children, by the hour subdued,
Thought only of the beautiful and good, —
No mischief lighting up the boyish face,
Nor on the girlish brow a single trace
Of teasing mirth, but, while all bickerings cease,
Were gliding homeward o'er the path of peace.

Well might the boatman ask again the song
Which in his spirit all day could prolong
The thought of God's good will and loving care
To all his children given everywhere;
And so again the melody went o'er
The waters as they sang "From Shore to Shore."

"Through storm or calm we glide along;
  We pass from shore to shore:
With blended tears and smiles we go
  To smile forevermore.
With love to God, and love to man,
  The spirit of the sky,
The young and old may calmly pass
  To angel-homes on high."

So sang contented hearts, which placed their trust
In One forever merciful as just;
And thus the chorus o'er the waters hied,
While Faith's bright vision saw beyond the tide.

> "From shore to shore, from shore to shore,
>   We're gliding on forever:
>  Keep watch and ward to guide and guard,
>   O Thou who slumberest never!"

# POEMS OF CHRISTIAN FAITH.

# POEMS OF CHRISTIAN FAITH.

## OUR HOME BEYOND THE TIDE.

[Written on receiving from a friend a beautiful engraving with the above title.]

OUR home is beyond the tide, friend,—
   Our home is beyond the tide,
Where the glorious city of light is seen
   Whose gates are open wide.
Through the golden streets of that city fair
   We soon shall pass along;
And a holy joy shall fill our hearts
   As we greet the shining throng
Who walk those streets through the endless day,
   Earth's dear ones side by side.
Oh, the bliss that awaits us when we reach
   Our home beyond the tide!

Our home is beyond the tide, friend,—
   Our home is beyond the tide,
Where the river of life, with its water bright,
   Is rolling deep and wide.
There the tree of life, with its fruit so fair,
   O'er the sparkling waters bends;

And beneath its shade, with unmeasured bliss,
    We shall meet our cherished friends.
Oh, we soon shall rest in those sacred bowers,
    Where no cynic our love shall chide,
And the saints' communion unhindered share,
    In our home beyond the tide!

Our home is beyond the tide, friend, —
    Our home is beyond the tide;
And though between us and that blissful shore
    The river of death may glide,
Yet its waters rough surging around our barks
    Can never our souls o'erwhelm:
We've hope for the anchor, and love for the breeze,
    And our Saviour at the helm.
We shall safely pass o'er the Jordan of death,
    To the land where the saints abide, —
To the home of the angels, the mansions of joy,
    To our home beyond the tide.

Our home is beyond the tide, friend, —
    Our home is beyond the tide;
And many a loved one, speeding there,
    Has vanished from our side.
For us will the voiceless Charon soon
    With his muffled oar draw nigh,
And bear us to meet the welcome sweet
    Of loved ones now on high.
How thrills the heart with the thought of tones
    Which ne'er from our hearts have died, —
Of the faces dear which we hope to greet
    In our home beyond the tide!

Our home is beyond the tide, friend, —
  Our home is beyond the tide;
And we must not sigh with a vain regret
  For the ills which here betide.
But oft, from the heights of faith sublime,
  Gaze far o'er the darksome wave,
And bless our God for the rest from care
  In the land beyond the grave.
The waves of sin surge no more round the Rock
  In the cleft of which we hide :
Oh, with longing hearts we wait the call
  To our home beyond the tide!

Our home is beyond the tide, friend, —
  Our home is beyond the tide ;
And we must not sigh for those earthly joys
  " Best Wisdom " hath denied.
For the thorns of earth, there are flowers in heaven;
  For its cares, there is long repose ;
For the vale of tears, there's the mount of joy
  Where the heart with rapture glows.
Then with loving hearts we will do His will
  In whose promise our hearts confide,
And patiently wait for our turn to reach
  Our home beyond the tide.

## MANKIND MOVES ONWARD.

"Mankind moves onward through the night of Time, like a procession of torch-bearers, and words are the lights which the generations carry. By means of these, they kindle abiding lamps beside the track which they pass; and some of them, like the stars, shall shine for ever and ever."

"Mankind moves onward through the night of Time,"
  On, though the stars are dim,
While through the darkness, like to Egypt's gloom,
  There comes no morning gleam.
Mankind moves onward; God is yet on earth;
And men grow worthier their immortal birth.

"Mankind moves onward through the night of Time;"
  For God is with us still,
In all our songs the key-note still to sound,
  And work his sovereign will:
That purpose, vast and glorious, yet shall stand,
Till this fair earth shall be Immanuel's land.

"Mankind moves onward through the night of Time;"
  And One — fair Bethlehem's Star —
His rugged path illumes with light of truth
  Sublime, and from afar,
Mingling with earth-born hopes, till, free from dross,
Through discipline, all else is counted loss.

"Mankind moves onward through the night of Time."
  Then faint not, O my soul!
Thou art thyself God's child among the rest,
  And thou shalt reach the goal;
And all thou lovest with thyself shall stand,
Forever safe from sin, at God's right hand.

---

## "AT EVENING TIME IT SHALL BE LIGHT."

DEAR, fainting pilgrim on Life's weary road,
  Lone voyager on Life's stormy, restless sea,
Faint not: though dark the lowering clouds may spread,
  At evening time it shall be light for thee.

Thus He who loves thy soul trod weary ways,
  Thus floated lonely on a starless sea;
Yet His the promise, — be to Him the praise! —
  "At evening time it shall be light for thee."

Now clouds and darkness are His children's lot;
  But soon a blissful dawn for them shall be, —
Glory beyond the stretch of mortal thought,
  Visions of beauty mortals may not see.

Hope on! unwavering, press thou through the gloom!
  The Cross must be thy pillar-cloud by day,
Thy blazing guard by night, till, nearing home,
  At evening time it shall be light for thee.

Faint not. The Voice which spake the word of yore,
    And was obeyed, o'er surging Galilee,
Speaks to thy soul in every stormy hour,
    "At evening time it shall be light for thee."

Dear voices hushed in Death's unpitying sleep,
    Thou mayest not hear this side the narrow sea:
They echo on that shore where none may weep;
    There shalt thou greet them when 'tis light for thee.

There shalt thou see the Crucified and Crowned,
    Thy chosen Master here, whose smile shall be
A full assurance that thine heart hath found
    At evening time 'twas surely light for thee.

---

## FARTHER ON.

Now the ills of earth surround us;
    Oft the storm-clouds hide the sun;
But, though dark the night around us,
    Day is breaking farther on:
        Farther onward,
    All the mists and clouds are gone.

Here the thorns with flowers are growing,
    Rough and weary is our path;
Gentle waters seldom flowing
    In the desert ways of earth:

Farther onward,
Sweet, immortal springs have birth.

Blossoms in our pathway springing,
    Fade, alas! too soon away;
Warblers, love's sweet chorus singing,
    Seek their rest ere close of day:
        Farther onward,
Flowers shall never know decay.

Farther on, the voice whose sweetness
    Cheered us ere it silent grew,
Tuned to more than seraph meetness,
    Sings those songs the angels know:
        Father onward,
We shall join the chorus too.

As we to our rest draw nearer,
    We shall pass through shady bowers,
And our feet, 'neath skies grown clearer,
    Press the fragrance from the flowers:
        Farther onward,
Strewing smoother paths than ours.

We will leave our Leader never;
    But we'll calmly onward press,
Till we dwell with him forever,
    'Mid supernal blessedness:
        Farther onward,
With the saints his name to bless.

Yet, till we, on high appearing,
    With the sin-freed hosts abide,

Welcome is each promise cheering,
  Telling us how deep and wide,
    Farther onward,
  Flows salvation's blissful tide.

---

## YOUR HEAVENLY FATHER KNOWETH.

CHILDREN of want and sorrow,
    Whose tears like rivers flow,
There is a glad to-morrow,
    Which ye shall ere long know.
Faint not beneath your burdens,
    Grieve not at thronging cares,
Ofttimes they are the guerdons
    Of liberty from snares.
In patience ever groweth
    Faith's strong and brilliant wings:
"Your heavenly Father knoweth
    Your need of all these things."

He knows that riches harden
    The God-forgetting heart,
So plucks from out your garden
    The plants which joy impart.
On heaven's hillsides glorious,
    Transplanted, they shall bloom,
Till, o'er your sins victorious,
    You reach that blessed home.

Salvation's trumpet bloweth :
  Hark ! while the message rings, —
" Your heavenly Father knoweth
  Your need of all these things."

Though marred your hopes so cherished,
  Though crossed your worldly schemes,
And on their stems have perished
  Your chosen plant's racemes ;
Though dark these providences,
  And heavy seems each cross, —
Towards heaven the soul advances
  By gain once counted loss.
Grief oft for heaven soweth,
  And Death the bright sheaves brings :
" Your heavenly Father knoweth
  Your need of all these things."

Each Marah is appointed ;
  There's no redundant thorn :
He spared not his Anointed,
  And we must follow on.
But, oh, there's consolation !
  Each fearful furnace-fire,
Each hour of desolation,
  Lifts the tried spirit higher,
On, toward where Life's stream floweth.
  Fold not your weary wings !
" Your heavenly Father knoweth
  Your need of all these things."

## THE DAY-STAR IN MY HEART.

I ASK not earthly pomp and power,
   Earth's riches or its joy;
For well I know Time's onward march
   Such glory will destroy:
But, O blest Saviour! grace impart,—
Oh light " the Day-Star in my heart"!

Amid the sorrows mortals know
   Along life's chequered way,
Where sweetest joys too soon are o'er,
   And brightest flowers decay,
One blessed boon, my God, impart:
Give me " the Day-Star in my heart"!

When sorrow's night, and sin's dark cloud,
   Seem hovering near my soul,
O thou who dost in earth and heaven
   O'er all things have control
Bid from my soul each cloud depart,—
Give me " the Day-Star in my heart"!

Then forth upon the wings of love
   To other hearts I'd speed,
And scatter there, with childlike faith,
   The precious gospel-seed,
Till penitential tears shall start,
And beams the Day-Star in each heart."

## THE EDEN ABOVE.

[A lady in Beverly presented to me, when about leaving that lovely spot to visit my native island, in 1860, a beautiful bouquet, asking that it should be preserved for a season, though the flowers composing it should wither; adding to the request the following excellent original stanza: —

"For Jesus disdains not, he counts not as loss,
   Those withered heart-blossoms Faith wreathes round his cross:
   More precious than lilies of Paradise, they
   In his own loving bosom are folded for aye!"

Her words suggested the following lines: —]

YES, thou art right! His loving heart,
   Which felt for human woe,
And suffered from keen sorrow's dart
   In ages long ago,
Still beats as warm, as true, as high,
   For every mortal grief, —
Still bends, like the o'er-arching sky,
   To whisper sweet relief.

No withered heart by sorrow seared,
   With hopes by grief destroyed,
But finds for it the cross upreared;
   In Christ, peace unalloyed.
Then, confident, thine offerings bring,
   O humble, contrite soul!
Thy presence bids the angels sing
   Where tides of glory roll.

The flowers upon each heavenly height
   Are ever sweet and fair;
But, to the tender Shepherd's sight,
   No blossoms are more dear

Than those which early fade on earth
   Beneath a clouded sky,
Too frail to bear the storm, the dearth
   Of heaven-born sympathy.

For such, celestial breezes blow,
   The "airs of Paradise;"
Such blossoms will, transplanted, grow,
   Perfecting, in the skies.
There flowers of faith immortal bloom,
   The buds of hope ne'er die,
And wreaths of love adorn the home
   Of spirits in the sky.

Then let no weary soul despair:
   A garden shall be found,
Where graces bloom whose fragrance here
   Oft makes earth hallowed ground.
Unfading there Love's rose shall bloom,
   Faith's floweret droop no more:
Oh when, dear Master, may our home
   Be found upon that shore!

---

## CHRIST'S INVITATION.

*"Come unto me all ye that labor and are heavy laden, and I will give you rest."*

"COME unto me, earth's weary ones!"
   The Saviour saith to-day;
"Come ye that, heavy-laden, sigh,
   Your burdens cast away.

Come to the Rock in Life's hot noon,
    And I will give you rest;
Come, weary pilgrim, hither come,
    And be forever blest."

Lord Jesus! now thy voice I hear,
    No longer I delay:
From earthly hopes and vain desires,
    My spirit turns away.
Thy voice, O Teacher most divine!
    With cadences so sweet,
Steals on my ear amid earth's din,
    And checks my wandering feet.

From cares which like the mountain waves
    Dash oft around my soul,
I turn, Lord of the world! to thee,
    Who canst the waves control.
I come to thee: speak thou again;
    Bid their wild tumult cease,
Till on my soul, like summer waves,
    They, breaking, murmur "Peace!"

Rest, rest in thee! my spirit longs
    For calm and sweet repose;
To have my soul a tranquil lake
    Whereon faith's lily grows.
I claim thy promise, gracious Lord!
    Thy love to weary me, —
Repenting, hoping, loving now,
    O Christ! I come to thee.

## THAT BETTER LAND.

IN that better land where the day dies not,
   And the flow'rets ne'er decay,
Where the angels pass on their errands bright,
   And the ransomed rejoice alway,
There the loving heart and the holy soul
Shall be free to act with but Love's control.

Oh! the bonds of earth shall be sundered there,
   And the soul shall freedom know;
And the music-tones of each heart sound forth
   With no note of human woe;
There the poor of earth with the crowned shall stand,
And no pride be known in that better land.

There the dwellers are free from the power of sin,
   And no tempter's wiles destroy;
There the ransomed dwell in that fold of love,
   And rejoice in each other's joy;
And the Lamb of God leads his happy band
In the verdant fields of that better land.

Oh! my heart throbs now with exultant thrill,
   As I muse on those joys in store
For the soul that trusts in a Saviour's love,
   And will seek to sin no more;
And by faith I'll clasp my Father's hand,
To be led by him toward that better land.

He may lead me down through the vales of grief,
  Or along joy's mountain-side ;
Yet I'll sing his praise, and I'll do his will,
  And I'll trust in the Crucified,
Till he bids me, free from all sin, to stand
On the joyful heights of that better land.

## VERBUM CONSOLATIONIS.

THOUGH the fairest plant in thy home's sweet
    bower
Is fading and failing, a frost-touched flower ;
Though the loved and cherished of long ago
Treads earth with a faltering step and slow,
And soon, alas ! the sweet memory
Of his love will alone be left to thee, —
Yet faint not, O disciplined one ! by the way,
But be thy Lord's promise forever thy stay.

He has pledged thee his strength when thine own
    should fail ;
He will shelter thy cot from the rising gale ;
He'll be thy Rock in Life's sultriest noon,
And thy kind Protector when all alone.
Then fear thou not, though the billows roar
Like the storm-dashed surf on an island shore ;
Fear not in his hand to place thine own,
Though thou treadest a path before unknown.

He will lead thee onward and upward still,
If thy heart says " Amen " to his holy will,
And the flames of thy fiercest furnace-fire
Will only help thee to mount up higher.
Though the angel Death shall invade thy bower,
And shall bear away thy loveliest flower,
Be thou calm; for he takes it to bloom on high,
Where the glorious blossoms ne'er shall die.

Oh! fear not to drink of the cup He bestows,
Who hath tasted the dregs of the chalice of woes.
In thy season of grief, as in his dark hour,
Lo! angels shall minister gently, with power
Thy grief to assuage, while the promises come
Reminding of heaven, that sorrowless home;
And thy spirit, exulting, at last shall arise,
To meet thy lost dear one again in the skies.

---

## THE COMING OF DEATH.

AS scents the war-horse battle-fields afar,
   So, Death, thy coming doth my soul perceive,
And, like a soldier at the trumpet's call,
   Girds on its armor, ready to receive
The summons to a conflict, Death, with thee,
   Secure of succor and of victory.

For angels wait to bathe my wounds, and place
   To parching lips the chalice of relief;
While Gabriel whispers, " Thou shalt overcome;
   The Master cometh, and the fight is brief."

And hark! the symphonies of heaven tell
  To dying Christians, "Fear not! all is well!"

And though I die, as early blossoms fall,
  Ere in my life the ripened fruits appear,
Eternal ages will the bud expand,
  Which found too soon the winter of Life's year.
I shall not die, but live, when Death for me
  Shall cut the earth-cords, and exclaim, "Be free!"

Oh let me meet him, then, in God's own time,
  Or soon, or late, as he, my Father, wills,
But meet him e'er with summer in my heart,
  Green fields of trust, and sympathy's glad rills,
Then, though the din of conflict sharp may ring,
  I'll die exclaiming, "Death hath lost its sting!"

Yet, if it please him, may his angel come
  A messenger with sweet and winning smile,
To bear my spirit to a land of rest,
  Where sin can ne'er my spotless robe defile!
Thy love, O Jesus! shall I there adore, —
  Because thou livest, live forevermore.

---

## DEATH AND VICTORY.

"Death is swallowed up in victory." — 1 COR. xv. 54.

TRIUMPHANT over sin and death,
  O Lord! thy children come,
With songs and everlasting joy,
  To share their promised home.

Wide open stand the glorious gates
　　Of thine eternal day;
And all the race shall enter in,
　　All share the victory.

No frightful phantom seemeth now
　　Thy messenger to be;
For, while he bears our friends away,
　　His angel-face we see.
He points us to the thorny path
　　Once by our Saviour trod,
And tells us, that through grief to joy
　　Shall pass each child of God.

Loud let our song of triumph be,
　　Till heaven's high arch shall ring:
The Grave hath lost its victory,
　　And Death hath lost its sting.
Glory to God! the angels sang;
　　His praise our souls respond:
We trust the love which placed us here
　　For all that lies beyond.

Unharmed, with angel guards around,
　　Perchance our cherished friends,—
In faith, O Lord! we calmly take
　　Whate'er thy mercy sends.
In life or death we would be thine;
　　In Christ from sin made free:
At last to know with rapturous joy
　　Death merged in victory.

## FREE THOUGHT.

I STAND beside the ever-rolling sea,
   And look afar across the waters blue;
The waters plash a pleasant tale to me,
   While Luna's silver line of light I view.

They tell of childhood's hours, when, by the deep,
   I wandered many an hour in thoughtful mood,
And solemn thoughts, that in young bosoms sleep,
   Came to my spirit like the breakers rude.

Then felt my soul the fetters which they know
   Who fear the future, trusting not in Him
Who bids the midnight change to morning's glow,
   And wipes the tears from eyes with sorrow dim.

I did not trust the great All-Father then,
   Nor dreamed, that, like the broad o'er-arching sky,
His love bent over all the sons of men,
   And freedom gave to those he called to die.

Now with unfettered gaze my faith can soar,
   And, eagle-eyed, behold the Father's love;
With joyful trust I now that God adore,
   Who rules on earth and in the heavens above.

Henceforth my soul is fetterless to range
   The boundless fields of thought, and pluck the
     flowers
Of faith and love, which angels interchange
   Amid the beauty of celestial bowers.

Free thought is his who owns a God supreme,
  Nor fears to trust where vision may not be,
Assured that in the end each noble dream
  Shall rich fulfilment find beyond Life's sea.

## LIGHT IN DARKNESS.

"Unto the upright there ariseth light in the darkness." — PSA. cxii. 4.

ONCE brooded o'er chaos the Spirit of God,
  Ere the fiat creative was echoed abroad;
But when the Divine One said, "Let there be light,"
The gladness of sunshine illumined the night.

When by the wayside sat Bartimeus the blind,
And cried, "Son of David, have mercy!" how kind
Was the gentle Redeemer who gave him his sight,
And out of lone darkness brought him to the light!

Where'er in the darkness God's servants did call, —
In dens with the lions, or in prison with Paul,
By rulers, by earthquake, or angel so bright, —
He brought them to freedom, changed darkness to
      light.

Then trusting thy mercy, believing thy word,
I'll struggle still onward and upward, my Lord: —
In trials or temptations my utt'rance shall be, —
"Give light in the darkness, O Saviour, to me!"

And when all the clouds of my earth-life pass by,
And I gaze with soul-vision unsealed to the sky,
Oh bid my freed spirit dwell henceforth with thee,
Where light, without darkness, forever shall be!

## THE STILL HOUR.

SWEET is the morning hour for praise,
   For trustful, earnest prayer,
When early birds their matins sing,
   And flowers perfume the air;
With strength renewed we rise to share
   The labors of the day,
While wisdom prompts us then to seek
   A sweet, "still hour" to pray.

When noon unclouded clothes the earth
   With emblematic light,
How oft the saint in faith beholds
   The land where all is bright!
And as his eye of faith shall see
   The glory yet to come,
Oh, may he not a "still hour" seek
   To muse on that bright home!

When twilight stillness round his path
   Proclaims the peace of God,
So sweetly shared by all who tread
   The path by Jesus trod, —

A thorny, yet an upward way,
　Where strength for toil is given, —
How sweet to claim that holy time,
　A lone, still hour for heaven!

And when the night with starry quiet,
　Or moonlit peace, shall come,
How welcome then a lone, "still hour,"
　For thoughts of that glad home
Towards which we trust our steps may tend,
　Though we in weakness tread
The rough, the labyrinthine path
　In which we oft are led!

O God! who in the hour of prayer
　Thy children here doth meet,
And lift the humble, contrite soul
　Which boweth at thy feet,
Give me to bend in reverent trust,
　And in thy love to share,
Whene'er, by day or night, I find
　The sweet, "still hour" of prayer!

---

## "GOD IS LOVE." — 1 John iv. 8.

AH! well might he upon Christ's bosom leaning,
　　The chosen few above,
Declare the truth, with zeal not overweening,
　That God, our God, is love.

Our God is love: his smile clothes earth in beauty,
    And robes it with delight;
And every heart that heeds the call of duty
    That love shall clothe in white.

Fair as the morning is the soul that loveth
    All things below, above,
Which he, the wise and holy One, approveth,
    Growing like him in love.

Our God is love, when fair and fragrant flowers
    Our daily pathway strew,
From his hand falling like the summer showers,
    Or like the gentle dew.

Aye, God is love, e'en when the crashing thunder
    Follows the lightning's stroke;
E'en when the ties of earth are rent asunder,
    And human hearts are broke.

Then let us trust him, and our love be showing
    By deeds of love to all,
Forever in his blessed likeness growing,
    Till we shall hear Death's call.

And when the parted veil opes to our vision,
    These truths all thought above,
Amid the bliss which fills the fields elysian,
    We'll echo, "God is love."

## THE LAST SUPPER.

It was an evening in the Holy Land,
   When Jesus gathered his disciples dear:
The Jews' Passover feast was nigh at hand,
   And they were met their Master's words to hear.
By his own hand the faithful few were fed;
   They drank the cup he gave them in that hour,
Nor saw the clouds that gathered round his head,
   Nor dreamed for them he'd bow to Cæsar's power.

Though on the hills around Jerusalem
   He oft had wandered with the chosen few,
And taught the holy prophecies to them
   Who ne'er before their deepest meaning knew,
They dreamed not of his death, but would have crowned
   The Meek and Lowly as a conquering King:
How could they bear to have their Master bound?
   How know he must o'ercome through suffering?

Upon his breast his best-loved follower leaned,
   While round him there Christ's arms in love were thrown:
How from such holy joy could John be weaned?
   How walk the paths of earth again alone?
Yet ere the morning must that Master sigh
   Beneath the shades of fair Gethsemane,
And while angelic ministers are nigh,
   Must bear, O sinner, sorrow's weight for thee!

The supper o'er, and Judas far away,
  His cheering words of love our Saviour spake,
Then prayed for all who near his cross should stay,
  Then bade the echoes with a hymn awake:
Thus prayer and music blended in that hour,
  With pathos, melody, and love divine,
Twin influences that o'er the soul have power
  A holy wreath around the heart to twine.

O Saviour blest! whene'er I bend the knee,
  Or sing the songs of Zion to thy praise,
I'll think, in love and faith, how thou for me
  Once trod, in holy grief, earth's weary ways.
And oh! as I shall at thy table bow,
  And taste the bread and wine with grateful heart,
How oft my tears must fall that such as thou
  Must die to win me to the better part!

## O RIVER OF GOD, ROLL ON!

[Suggested by a sermon preached by Rev. J. C. Foster, Oct. 13, 1861, in First Baptist Church, Beverly, from the text, "There is a river the streams whereof shall make glad the city of God."]

O RIVER of God! roll on e'ermore.
    On the bright and blissful tide
Have our saints now safe on the heavenly shore
    Been borne to the Saviour's side.
Our loved ones shine in their robes of white,
    All cleansed in thy crystal stream,
In the image of him they love, more bright
    Than the sheen of a fairy dream.

O river of God! roll on: in thee
   Exulting, I'd bathe my soul,
Till my sin-stained spirit was pure and free,
   And each thought knew love's control.
Salvation is in thy gentle flow:
   Thy waters have power to heal;
Their taste, O God! bid my soul to know,
   Their virtues my heart to feel.

O river of God! roll on, and still,
   Like the river the prophet saw,
May thy waters deepen, thy channels fill,
   Till the world can hold no more!
And the timid saint may God inspire
   With the strength earth may not know,
To swim when thy waters, rising higher,
   His head would overflow!

O river of God! roll on, roll on,
   In thy channels broad and deep;
With tide unebbing still flow on
   While the nations wake and sleep.
O'er thy flowery banks hang the healing leaves,
   On the trees so large and fair,
Whose fruit the voyager with joy receives,
   And angels' food may share.

O river of God! roll on, roll on,
   Till thy waves shall skirt each shore,
Till the wide, wide world shall be fruitful made
   By thy fertilizing power,
Till the far-off heathen no more shall bow
   Where a Ganges in vain may glide,

But wash from his soul earth's sin and woe
    In thy glad and sparkling tide.

O river of God! roll on, roll on,
    Thy waves no bar shall know;
Flow on till the break of the endless morn;
    Unhindered, through Time, still flow!
And when thy vast waters the sea shall gain,
    God's ocean of love and joy,
High praises shall sound far o'er the bright main,
    Whose echoes no more shall die.

## REJOICE EVERMORE.

REJOICE that the day of thy life is begun;
    Rejoice though the night of the grave cometh on;
For both must be known ere, on heaven's bright shore,
Thou wilt sing with the angels, and sigh nevermore.

Rejoice though the tempest-cloud darkens above,
Though thy hopes may be blighted, and crushed be thy love: '
Those hopes yet will blossom, the storm will be o'er,
And thy love be returned where they love evermore.

Rejoice though, through weakness, sometimes thou may'st fall:
For the God who would save thee still rules over all;

The Shepherd still ranges the dark mountains o'er,
To gather the lost, that they sin nevermore

Rejoice! e'en afflictions are joys in disguise,
And tears shall but banish the dust from thine eyes.
Why go about sighing for joys that are o'er?
In God's garner of bliss there are sheaves evermore.

All grief shall depart; and the sorrows of Time
Shall seem but the echoes of some far-off chime;
And the thorns that grew thick in our pathways of
    yore
Shall change to the flowers that shall fade nevermore.

Rejoice, then, rejoice! for all sorrow and sin,
All the cares of our earth-life, its trouble and din,
All the conflicts of Right with the Wrong, shall be
    o'er,
And the victors o'er evil rejoice evermore.

Rejoice! where the angels their white wings unfold,
Through the gateways of pearl, o'er the pavements
    of gold,
Our glad feet shall pass, all our journeyings' o'er,
And we'll rest in the land where they weep never-
    more.

Rejoice! for the souls it was bliss here to know
Shall greet us again when from hence we shall go;
And the songs that together we'll sing on that shore
Shall have for their chorus, "Rejoice evermore."

## A VISION BY FAITH.

THAT land of delight, my soul's Beulah, I see,
    As I think of thy home, blessed Saviour! and thee;
And my spirit is longing that land to behold,
Of whose glory and beauty the half was ne'er told.

It needs not the sunshine all glorious and bright;
It needs not the moonbeams which beautify night;
For each hillside is lit by the glory of God,
And the Lamb lights the vales where the ransomed have trod.

There the saints I have loved, whose bright crowns are now won,
And whose work for the Master was faithfully done,
Will gather to meet me, with smiles as of yore,
Where my bark shall be moored, as I step on that shore.

There a mother whose form I've ne'er consciously seen,
But who looked in my infant face, loving, I ween,
Will welcome her storm-tossed and travel-worn child,
To a haven of rest, to a land undefiled.

O vision of glory! still linger with me,
Till I float calmly forth on eternity's sea, —
Till I near the blest harbor, and Jesus shall say,
"Cast anchor, O voyager! in heaven's broad bay."

## A MORNING WITHOUT CLOUDS.

FEW are the mornings that are cloudless here,
　Few the glad hours that know no gloomy shade;
But one bright morning will at last appear
Radiant as if with angel-robes arrayed.

The morn that breaks upon the ransomed soul
When from the bonds of flesh and sin set free,
While Passion's waves no longer wildly roll,
And the frail bark floats not on Sorrow's sea, —

The cloudless morn! it ushers in the day,
Glad, bright, and beautiful, that ne'er shall end:
How blest are they who hope to greet its ray,
And ceaseless ages in its light to spend!

Hearts that are throbbing o'er some hope deferred,
Eyes that are dim with weeping all the day
O'er homes grown desolate, have gladly heard,
And patient wait the hour to pass away.

Waiting beside the river! — soon to speed
Across the billows to the land of rest, —
The home for all God's children, where, indeed,
The loving spirit shall at last be blest.

O morning without clouds! my spirit-bark
Is waiting now beside the solemn sea.
Come in thy brightness! light each pathway dark,
And give the radiant gladness now to me.

I do not fear to greet thee : I have seen
Pale faces glow beneath thy wondrous light,
And on the silent lips a smile serene ;
And I would follow to the land of light.

Break then, O cloudless morn ! break thou for me,
Whene'er my earthly toils and griefs are o'er ;
Then, with exultant joy, I'll cross Death's sea,
And greet my crowned ones on Life's farther shore.

---

## LIGHT AND LIBERTY.

"THE light that lighteth every man,"
      How fair it shone
When o'er the hills of Palestine
      One star alone
Gleamed with a radiance that can never die
Till God's dear children reach their home on high!

The liberty wherewith our Lord
      Doth make men free,
A thought of which awakes the song
      Of jubilee !
How doth the cross symbolic prove
Of freedom, based on perfect love !

O Light and Liberty ! sweet words,
      Which in this hour
To stir the faithful-hearted in our land
      Have magic power.

Christ hath proclaimed them both: their dawn
Came with the hour when the Christ-child was born.

Thank God for *light* on human pathways thrown, —
    The truth's glad ray;
Thanks for the *liberty* from sin's dread bonds
    In endless day,
While mortals join the angel-anthem sweet,
And sing the glorious work of Christ complete.

Then light and liberty shall be secured
    To all the race;
And the glad tidings which the shepherds heard
    Shall then give place
To victors' shouts upon the heavenly plains,
And the glad acclamation, "Jesus reigns!"

---

## NO MORE TEARS.

"The Lord God shall wipe the tears from off all faces." — Isa. xxv. 8.
"God shall wipe away all tears from their eyes." — Rev. vii. 17.

TEARS shall not fall in the world of joy
    Towards which our steps are tending.
Our crowns shall be gold without alloy,
    Our songs have no grief-tone blending.

Tears shall not glisten in eyes we love,
    Our hearts for their dear sakes grieving,
When they reach the land of light above,
    This world of shadows leaving.

Tears shall not moisten the cheek we press
   With the kiss of friendly greeting:
All free from sorrow, the fond caress
   That awaits us in that meeting,

Where the promise fulfilled to us shall be,
   And tears are wiped from all faces;
Where the heart that throbbed so wearily
   Shall find of grief no traces.

A little while through the night fall tears;
   But the glad bright day is dawning:
Our sins shall vanish, our griefs, our fears, —
   Joy comes with the coming morning.

## THE FEAST OF LIFE.

"THE feast of life is sweet:
   I am no weary guest;"
But joyful at my Saviour's feet
   I heed his high behest.
I eat the living bread,
   I quaff the draught divine;
And love within my heart is shed,
   And light doth round me shine.

'Tis sweet to taste his love
   Whom cross-crowned Calvary knew;
Sweet to look hopefully above,
   Where soon we hope to go.

My soul feeds on thy word,
   And strength receives from thee:
I weary not of thee, my Lord;
   Oh, weary not of me!

When in thy presence blest,
   From sorrow free I stand,
See thee with John upon thy breast,
   And Paul at thy right hand,
Oh, with exultant joy,
   My Master, I shall sing!
Thy praise shall be my soul's employ,
   Till heaven's high arch shall ring.

For, at the heavenly feast
   Where thy new wine is poured,
I ne'er shall be a weary guest,
   Since thou art there, my Lord.
Sweet to my sin-freed soul
   The bliss I then shall share;
Sweet are the foretastes now to me,
   While yet a pilgrim here.

Like glimpses fair and bright
   Seen through the morning mist,
So to my faith's cloud-piercing sight
   Appears the land of rest.
Calmly I wait thine hour,
   Yet stand with ready feet,
To heed thy call to that bright shore,
   Thy face, my Lord, to greet.

A pilgrim weak am I,
   And oft from thee I stray;

But oh, I would reach yonder sky,
  I would be thine alway!
Still at the feast of life,
  For strength let me sit down,
Till victor, through thee, in the strife,
  I wear the conqueror's crown.

---

## NEARER.

NEARER? yes, I'm nearer now
  The silent, solemn sea
Which rolls between my weary heart,
  Jerusalem! and thee.
I'm nearer to the boatman now:
  He soon will shout "Away!"
Oh! to my home beyond the sea
  I'm nearer every day.

Some days are dreary, some bring tears,
  Some undefined regret;
While on some golden hours, thank God!
  Hope's radiance lingers yet.
But whether days be dark or bright,
  The moments swift or slow,
Time stops not in his steady flight,
  And onward still we go.

On the green hillsides of yon shore
  Our loved ones calmly wait;
And angel forms to welcome us
  Half open heaven's gate.

Oh, rapturous thought! that rest, sweet rest,
   Will soon to us be given,
Since every hour the child of God
   Is drawing nearer heaven.

O Saviour! as we thus draw near
   The throne, the crystal sea,
The holy throng, the heavenly choir,
   We're drawing *nearer thee*, —
Nearer the hour when we, whose feet
   The olive slopes ne'er trod
Or shores of far-off Galilee
   Where walked the Son of God,

Shall see his face, shall hear his voice,
   Shall touch that pierced hand,
And on the brow, thorn-crowned for us,
   Shall gaze, and silent stand.
Oh, thought to cheer my weary way,
   With welcome radiance come!
Let me remember that each day
   I'm drawing nearer home!

## JOYS TO COME.

THE joys of earth are manifold,
   Our every footstep greeting;
And birds and flowers, and hills and streams,
   In beauty we are meeting.

Yet earth is not our only home,
  The thought brings sweet emotion:
Our brightest joys we hope to share
  Beyond Life's stormy ocean.

We love our glad green earthly homes,
  Our bright and sparkling waters,
The rich communion here we hold
  With earth's fair sons and daughters;
But oh! that home we hope to gain,
  Far, far above the mountains,
Has greener fields and bluer skies,
  And purer, sweeter fountains.

Beyond the grave, where not a soul
  By mem'ries sad is haunted,
But where the wondrous healing-tree
  By Life's fair stream is planted,
There is our home, with joy more rare
  Than told in Eastern story;
And Christ's dear smile its light shall give
  Through all that realm of glory.

## "WE SHALL BE LIKE HIM."

"WE shall be like him!" Here the mists of sin
  Oft cloud the brightness which might beam within,
And, by our souls reflected, bid them shine
With likeness to their Master, loved, divine.

But there unclouded shall our vision be;
Each soul unhindered, heaven's light shall see;
And glory unimagined gild the day
Which dawns for us when earth is passed away.

"We shall be like him!" Here we strive in vain.
Sin mars the work we hoped would fair remain;
And when some virtue rises in the soul,
Pride scales the mount, and overthrows the whole.

But *there* we shall be purified from sin,
Made beautiful without and glorious within;
And, humble like our Master, bow us down
In lowly reverence to receive a crown.

"We shall be like him!" Oh, what rapturous bliss
For Christian hearts is in a pledge like this!
To be like thee, our Lord, is to be free
From every tie which holds us now from thee.

It is to dwell where love shall reign supreme,
And beauty shall excel our fairest dream,
And holiness, a glowing sun, shall shine, —
Rich synonymes which speak of the Divine.

"We shall be like him" when we take the crown
Where weights of bliss shall bow each spirit down.
O soul of mine! be patient till the hour
Which strikes the end of sin's terrific power.

*Then* let praise be given, Lord, to thee;
For thou alone the captive soul can free.
The *bliss* of being like thee shall be mine;
But all the *glory*, blessed Lord, is thine!

## THE PURPOSE OF CREATION.

*"Thou hast created all things, and for thy pleasure they are and were created." — Rev. iv. 2.*

YES, for thy pleasure, Lord,
    All things in heaven and all in earth were made, —
Morn's welcome light, and evening's holy shade,
The many stars that gem the midnight sky,
The bright-hued flowers that all earth beautify,
The grand old forest monarchs in their pride,
The mighty ocean, fathomless and wide, —
    All for thy pleasure, Lord.

    Yes, for thy pleasure, Lord,
The mountains crested with eternal snows,
The glaciers that in far-off ages froze,
Each wondrous stratum of the solid earth,
And every form of life that e'er had birth, —
All for thy pleasure were created, Lord:
Thou call'dst them to existence with thy word,
    All for thy pleasure, Lord.

    Man for thy pleasure, Lord,
Was in thy image made, when light broke o'er
Those Eden tree-tops in the days of yore;
And though that death which is but second birth
Must be a portion of the sons of earth,
Yet surely not to die forevermore
Did'st thou make him who lords creation o'er,
    But for thy pleasure, Lord.

And thy great pleasure, Lord, —
God of the good, the beautiful, the true!
God whom the angels pure adoring view, —
Is, that the life thou gavest be sanctified,
And thy dear Son, who for the race hath died,
Shall lead at last, where sweet, soft waters glide,
The faithful flock, and each stray lamb beside:
Such is thy pleasure, Lord.

# POEMS OF FRIENDSHIP.

# POEMS OF FRIENDSHIP.

## TO MABELLE.

[In response to anonymous lines inscribed to the writer.]

"Grief knits two hearts in closer bonds than happiness ever can; and common sufferings are far stronger links than common joys." — LAMARTINE.

"Grace be with all who love our Lord Jesus Christ in sincerity and truth." — ST. PAUL.

"The human heart is like heaven, — the more angels the more room." — FREDERIKA BREMER.

MABELLE! friend, I now shall call thee,
   Though perchance I never see
Thy face, 'mid the dear ones hanging
   "On the walls of memory."
Mabelle, as a friend draw nearer,
   And reveal thyself to me.

They who can in tuneful numbers
   Touch with joy the poet's lyre;
They upon whose spirit-altars
   Burns the poet's holy fire, —
Surely they can ne'er be strangers,
   Members of the same sweet choir.

Friend! — nay, more, I call thee *sister*, —
   Suffering, human hearts can bind,
In a union purer, stronger,
   Than if mutual joys intwined
Those who, in the bonds of friendship,
   Sweet communion oft may find.

Oft have I at sorrow's fountain
   Quaffed the bitter draught with tears,
Struggled in the night of suffering
   With besetting human fears,
Said " Farewell " with aching spirit
   To the loved of many years.

So I hail thee as a sister,
   To my heart by sorrow bound;
And I mourn with thee thy dear ones,
   Resting 'neath each lowly mound,
For their sakes grown holy. precious, —
   Thine own consecrated ground.

More than this! my spirit claims thee
   As a sister, Mabelle, now,
Since, beneath the rod of chastening,
   Meekly doth thy spirit bow,
And the mark of a disciple
   Angels see upon thy brow.

I love all who love my Saviour,
   Whatso'er their creed or name,
Asking but that their devotion
   Rise a pure, perennial flame,
Daily deeds of love attesting
   Whence the sacred incense came.

So I hail thee as a sister,
   In the bonds that shall endure;
And my heart with thine is beating,
   Keeping time forevermore,
Hoping oft again to meet thee
   Here, and on Life's farther shore.

Yes, the spirit, ever growing,
   Vacant chambers e'er shall know,
Without sending forth a tenant
   Of the spirit long ago,
Like those mansions where the ransomed
   Pass in gladness to and fro.

In the soul each day expanding,
   Fast the "many mansions" grow;
Some of which the death-sealed tenant,
   Some for friends still here below,
Some for angels, and the saved ones
   Of the land to which we go.

Yes: I have a "vacant chamber."
   Thou shalt be a welcome guest,
If my love, for Christ's sake given,
   Can make thee a moment blest,
Whispering the eternal password,
   Mabelle, "Enter there and rest."

## JE VOUS REMERCIE.

THANKS for the gift whose gilded edges glow,
    Whose pencilled landscapes far-off beauty show:
For years to come, if years to come be mine,
Friendship's sweet halo shall around it shine;
And every piece shall speak to me of thee,
Who kindly sped the welcome gift to me.

I shall recall the mention of thy sire,
Revered and reverend, who, with holy fire
From shrines all holy, spoke to men of God,
And beckoned them to tread the path he trod,
Whose flowers and thorns to virtue led the soul,
Whose end was joy while pauseless ages roll.

When from these cups the Oriental draught,
With eager haste, my willing lips shall quaff,
Sweet as the cane whose essence shall be there
Will come the memory of thy friendly care;
And in the harmless cup which only cheers,
I'll drink to thee, — God bless thy future years!

God give thee health, and grant that e'er on thee
Each wrinkle shall a line of beauty be,
Which Time may place upon the mortal brow,
Till death shall bid thy soul with seraphs bow,
And the long pilgrimage of earth be done,
Life's final battle fought, and victory won.

God bless both thee and thine till we shall drink
A sweeter draught than earth's from the fair brink
Of that fair river flowing soft, serene,
Where healing leaves and precious fruit are seen,
And all the sin-freed host rejoice for aye
In the pure splendor of celestial day.

## BIRTHDAY STANZAS.

MOTHER, my heart is with thee now:
I fain at thy dear knee would bow,
And feel thy kiss upon my brow.

Another birthday thou hast known;
And forty-seven suns have shone
On thee, my mother dear, mine own.

Thank God, my spirit says, for thee, —
"God's 'bodied blessing" e'er to me:
Oh would that I thy face could see!

I may not clasp thy hand to-night;
But I may seek, with thee, the light,
That I may walk with thee in white.

Hope looketh to a fairer shore;
And Faith oft views its green fields o'er,
Where we shall rest forevermore; —

Where the great ocean, wild and free,
Shall sever not my steps from thee,
And we shall both our Saviour see.

Pray on, loved mother, for thy child,
That Christ may shield when storms are wild,
And keep my spirit undefiled.

And I will ask, that, sin-forgiven,
My "mother Ellen" enter heaven,
Wearing the crown for which she's striven.

And when the angels gather round,
Thine escort o'er the hallowed ground,
By thy dear side may I be found!

## SIXTIETH BIRTHDAY OF F. BARDEN.

WE'RE gathered here to greet one friend to-night
    With loving words and kindly clasp of hand,
To say that we are glad the Reaper Death
    Hath left this ripened sheaf with us to stand:
Too oft he gathers fairest flowers, and leaves
To long, dark years the hearts he thus bereaves.

But we are gathered, too, with grateful hearts
    For all the bounties of that boundless love

Which gives us health and friends and every gift
    To win our hearts, and bid us look above
To that fair land where we shall meet again
The loved and lost of earth, all free from sin.

We think of such to-night: we cannot meet
    In friendly converse with the dear ones left,
Without some thoughts of those who earlier passed,
    And left our hearts to mourn, that, thus bereft,
We must walk onward through Life's lengthened day,
Nor hope to meet them till *we* pass away.

Yet while sweet thoughts of blessings that have flown,
    Which brighten with the swiftly rolling years,
Still linger in our hearts like music tones,
    We bless our God for all that Life endears, —
For friends remaining still upon this shore,
Till God's call comes to sail the great sea o'er.

O friend! whose birthday we remember now
    With grateful hearts that God hath sent thee here,
To tread the ways of virtue and of truth,
    And many a heart to bless, and path to cheer,
We come to-night to clasp thy hand in love,
And ask for thee the blessing from above.

We thank the Guiding Mercy that hath led
    Thy feet to tread in Wisdom's better way,
And hath thine industry and labor blest
    With good success as we behold this day;
But most of all hath helped thee well to know,
That noble deeds assist the soul to grow.

God bless thee still, and bless with thee the friend,
   Long years ago thy loved and chosen bride,
And still by mercy spared to tread Life's path
   E'en to thy sixtieth birthday, at thy side:
God spare you, with each present, absent friend,
To meet full oft ere life on earth shall end.

And when we part to meet no more below;
   When, one by one, we're summoned to the skies,—
Love's golden chain will still unbroken be,
   And to our Father's house we all shall rise:
Let this thought make more glad this festive hour,
That we are subjects of God's sovereign power.

Nor yet his *Power* alone, but Sovereign LOVE,
   Which sees the falling sparrow, counts each hair,
Guides every star through space, and deems no soul
   Beyond the sweep of his paternal care.
He will be with us till our lives shall end,
And in his home, at last, join friend with friend.

---

## WHAT SHALL I WISH FOR THEE?

WHAT shall I wish for thee? long life on earth,
   Or wealth, or pleasure, or the magic power
To wield a sceptre over human hearts,
   And make them bow to thee through Life's short
      hour?

Not so: the joys of earth will fade away;
   Its power and pleasure are but bubbles bright;
The longest life may not the happiest be,
   And riches on proverbial wings take flight.

But I will wish thee joy at God's right hand,
   When earthly scenes have faded from thy view, —
A crown, a harp, a victor palm, for thee,
   Where dwell the loving and the pure and true.

May all thou lovest greet thee on the shore
   Where God each earth-born tear shall wipe away!
Through future ages may thy pathway gleam
   In all the splendor of eternal day!

---

## ALBUM STANZAS.

### TO E. R.

I GIVE thee greeting as a kindred soul;
    For throbs with thine,
In the pulsations will may not control,
    This heart of mine.

May we walk onward, side by side in love,
    Till one shall go
To join the life-crowned, joyous host above,
    And leave below

A waiting spirit, which its wings may plume
      For upward flight,
To the fair region where sweet flowerets bloom
      In cloudless light!

There may we meet, sweet friend, to part no more,
      From sorrow free,
With all God's children on that brighter shore,
      Beyond Time's sea!

## FAREWELL TO "CARLETON."

"CARLETON," farewell! I clasp thy friendly hand
  This side the sea no more:
Yet with a smile I spoke the farewell word,
  And saw thee start for that far-distant shore;
For well I knew that 'twould be joy to thee,
To tread those shores beyond the heaving sea.

Farewell! thine early hope hath blossomed now:
  Its fruit, to thee and thine,
Shall sweeter be than Eschol's clusters fair,
  As ye shall roam beside the sparkling Rhine,
Or wander in old England's halls of pride,
Or climb, awe-struck, the Alpine mountain side.

Farewell to her who travels at thy side,
  Thy second self, so dear:
With tender, loving thoughts of by-gone hours,
  I bid ye go, and wander far from here.

Your work is one, your hearts in concord beat:
God guide you both, till we again shall meet.

Farewell! in hope, I bid you both to go.
　　What though you ne'er return
To this dear land for which you've labored so,
　　You shall be blessed by all that you shall learn,
And scatter seeds of truth as oft before,
And bless new friends upon that foreign shore.

We who remain will hail each earnest word
　　You send us from afar,
Which tells how God is working in those lands,
　　And 'mid those troubled nations where ye are,
And pray the while that you may both be spared
To hail the hour when Peace shall be declared.

Our work will all be finished by and by:
　　We'll cross a wider sea.
Then shall we meet, nor speak the parting word
　　Through all the ages of eternity:
Each fond misgiving Hope's glad beams dispel.
We can afford to part a while: farewell!

## THEY SAY THAT I LOVE THEE.

THEY say that I love thee, that thou art to me
　　As the gods to the heathen, — a fair deity.
And they tell but the truth when they say thou art
　　dear;
For, as blossoms so fair in the morn of the year,

Do I oft hail thy presence, — a star on my way;
And thy smile is as welcome as bright, sunny May.

Oh, yes, I do love thee! and welcome to me
Comes thy sweet, merry laugh, like a song o'er the sea.
Thou cheerest my pathway like music; thy smile
Doth oft from its sorrows my spirit beguile:
Then why should I not write thy name on my heart,
And pray that our spirits no earth-power may part?

They say that I love thee: oh! why should I not
Rejoice, when I meet in Life's desert a spot
So like an oasis my spirit would rest,
And in each friendly shade for a season be blest;
Since shadows oft gather in earth's narrow sky,
We should bask in all sunshine which God may bring nigh.

They say that I love thee: they think that I bow
At the shrine of the earth-born to offer my vow.
Yes, truly, but only through loved ones to pay
My homage to him whom we honor alway.
In Jesus I love my heart's chosen alone,
And the Saviour of sinners sits on my heart's throne.

May he bless to our spirits the love that we share,
And fill our earth-lives with love, labor, and prayer,
Till he crowns us his own in the mansions above,
The home of the souls he hath here sought to love,
Where our prayers are for praises exchanged evermore,
And all labor for rest on the heavenly shore!

## MEMENTO LINES TO A FRIEND.

SHALL I wish thee joy, or sorrow,
   In thine earthly path, my friend?
Joy alone would but enervate,
   Sorrow break where it should bend.

God will blend them as his wisdom
   Knoweth how thy soul to keep:
Earthly changes all are needful;
   Heaven is nearest those who weep.

In God's hands thy future leaving,
   I for thee but crave this boon,
That, where'er thy feet may wander,
   Thou shalt never walk alone.

On the mountain-tops of gladness,
   Or along the peaceful plain,
Or when treading grief's dark valley,
   May thy Lord with thee remain!

Following him with thoughtful spirit,
   Thou shalt reach the home above,
Where the soul can bear the brightness,
   'Mid the joy of perfect love.

# SONNETS.

# SONNETS.

## WILLIAM H. PRESCOTT.

LIKE some bright star his early promise shone;
    Then, like that star eclipsed, went out a while,
Till Wisdom Infinite, the path alone
    Which he should tread in joy marked with a smile.
Admiring readers see that Wisdom now,
    And thank that Power that wisely thus ordained,
While laurel wreaths they twine around his brow
    Who pressed undaunted towards the prize he gained.
Then with the plaintive notes of mourning hearts,
    One loud, triumphant peal must mingle too,
That, ere such genius from our earth departs,
    Its glorious trophies lit that star anew,
And "Prescott the Historian" stands beside
The Judge and Colonel who with honor died.

## GEORGE WASHINGTON.

COME, patriot hearts! and bring a tribute now
    To him, our country's loved and honored sire;
Come, twine another wreath around his brow,
    And higher lift the flame upon his pyre.
Oh! let our nation guard his sacred dust,
    And keep unchanged the home his presence blessed.
America alone should keep that trust,
    And thus be true to honor's high behest.
Like some lone mountain 'mid a desert drear,
    Mount Vernon towers in moral grandeur now:
Still grand, but less alone, would it appear,
    Could all the admiring train around it bow,
And claim of him who'd honor e'en a throne,
His memory, his home, his dust, their own.

## TO A FRIEND IN SADNESS.

DOTH sadness o'er thy spirit sometimes steal,
    And darken all thy hours with doubt and fear,
As when the sun, while planets seem to wheel
    Across his disc, is darkened to us here?
Or as when clouds depart, which long o'erhung
    The earth with leaden visage, we rejoice;
So does thy spirit, in the song thou'st sung,
    Find brightness giving gratitude a voice?

Whate'er to-day thy lot may seem to oe,
  With thorns or flowerets strewn, beloved friend,
This is the prayer which I shall breathe for thee, —
  That thou be faithful till this life shall end;
Faithful to Him who trod the path of woe,
That thou shouldst share those joys the ransomed know.

---

## SUGGESTED BY THE CAPTURE OF CHARLESTON.

O GOD of battles! On the bended knee,
  With smiles of joy that may not be repressed,
Grateful and hopeful, now we come to thee,
  We whom thy goodness hath so richly blessed.
Our country's " crimson stripes and fadeless stars "
  Above once " startled Sumter " proudly wave :
Behold, through gates which Liberty unbars,
  Come peace to us, and joy to every slave.
Let the full tide of our rejoicings flow,
  Forever mingled with our grateful praise.
Thou reignest on earth; thy power the nations know.
  Peace is his portion who thy law obeys ;
And blessed peace must crown this war-purged land,
Now truth and freedom go forth hand in hand.

## A WINTER SONNET.

THE winter winds are fiercely howling now
    In wrath around my cherished " sea-side bower,"
As if to bid my spirit meekly bow,
    And own the storm-king's might the greater power.
Not so: the genial sun is coming fast,
    The radiant glory of the summer day.
The reign of terror then will soon be past;
    And peace returning shall call forth our praise.
Thus ever must all doubts and fears depart
    Which chill our spirits as a wintry clime,
When Love, which conquers fear and death, the heart
    Makes glad and bright like hours of summer-time.
Let Love, then, reign supreme within my breast,
Faith, Hope, and Charity shall make me blest.

## TO JOANNA QUINER.

AND this is woman's work! this noble brow,
    These "features cast in Nature's finest mould,"
Thy skill evoked from out the damp, dull clay,
    To gladden loving hearts as they behold.
Thine is a noble mission, thus to spare
    From dark oblivion many a noble head.

The casket whence the priceless gem is gone
    May still be dear for memories yet unfled;
And thou art favored thus to shadow forth,
    Though dimly as thou thinkest, woman's power,
Her talent, genius, intellectual might,
    And holy sympathy, her precious dower.
God mould thy spirit till like him thou art,
And stamp his sacred image on thy heart.
    1860.

## ON SEEING A BUST BY MISS QUINER.

WITH sudden thought I paused beside the bust;
    And Cowper's touching words unbidden rose,
" Oh that those lips had language!" and those eyes
    Lit with the fire of soul might once unclose!
Yet not with Uzziah sacrilege would I
    Seek aught beyond the will of love supreme,
Nor sigh, Pygmalion-like, that life be given
    To aught of human mould, though fair it seem.
Man may the marble shape, the plastic clay
    Mould, till the thinking brain, the throbbing heart,
Seem only needed to perfect the whole:
    The breath of life God only can impart.
Thanks for those powers which link us to the skies,
Though ne'er to our Creator's height we rise.
    1860.

## FOR THE GRAVE OF MRS. A. A. FOSTER.

JUNE'S roses still in beauty round me blow;
    Their fragrance fills the languid summer air;
While once again to thy dear grave I go,
    And lay my simple but love-offering there.
I go to look on one thou lovedst well, —
    Upon her form, robed for the silent grave.
Her soul hath sped away with thee to dwell,
    Far from all sin, beyond the chilly wave.
I gave her kindly message for thine ear;
    And she will tell thee, precious friend, I know,
How green thy memory in our spirits here,
    How much we long where thou art gone, to go;
And, when our ties to earth like hers are riven,
    We'll gladly meet you both in yon bright heaven.

READING, MASS., June 19, 1865.

## LIBERTY *VERSUS* ROMANISM.

[A sonnet respectfully inscribed to Rev. Arthur B. Fuller, whose recent excellent sermons with the above title suggested its composition.]

DOTH Freedom dwell where Papal rule is known?
"Nay!" History answers with a clarion voice,
Dark Superstition binds those votaries down
Who blindly of her guidance make sad choice.

The Old World groans to-day beneath the weight
Of burdens laid on her by Papal power,
Which seemeth e'er to pledge perpetual hate
To light and liberty, man's precious dower.
Say! shall these fetters our brave freemen bind,
And Popery's banners wave o'er Freedom's soil?
Not so, while truth and valor here are joined,
And true hearts for the holy cause may toil.
The parasite its strong support would kill,
And Rome with woe our native land would fill.

## FLOWERS.

[On beholding the beautiful flowers sent by Mr. Bela Whiton to the Universalist Church, Hingham Mass., on the day of my ordination.]

O SWEET, bright flowers! I welcome you to be
    Upon God's altar in the winter hour,
An emblem of the land beyond Life's sea,
    Where flowers e'er bloom, and storm-clouds never lower.
'Tis well that here your fragrance should be spent,
    Where human voices utter praise to God,
To teach us that our powers all are lent,
    And must be given back to him, our Lord.
O beauteous blossoms! to our hearts ye speak
    Of absent loved ones on the shining shore;
And thanks are due the hand which thus can wake
    The chords of memory till our spirits soar,
On Faith's bright wings, to hail the precious band
    Who wait our coming in the better land.

# POEMS OF PATRIOTISM.

And that as it grows, so light may dawn
   On the paths so dark before,

And the bondman find that the chains are broke,
   That no slave breathes our air,
And that in the anthems of the free
   The black man's voice hath share, —
Not the low, deep bass of a gathering storm,
   Or the heart-wrung minor tone,
But the glad, free notes of a happy soul,
   To whom Freedom's joys are known.

It will come, 'twill come, that glorious day,
   When the slave will not be found,
With a crouching fear or a muttering wrath,
   On Freedom's blood-stained ground!
Sing on, thou poet, of "furnace fires"!
   Still hoping, I sing with thee:
Hallelujah! the black man standeth *now*,
   War freed, 'neath that live-oak tree.
1861.

## SOLDIER, REST!

[A tribute laid on the coffin of Jonathan Cook of Reading, Mass., who was starved in a rebel prison, so that he died just after being exchanged. His body was brought to his native place, and funeral services held in the Universalist place of worship, Rev. E. A. Eaton officiating.]

SOLDIER, rest! thy march is done;
   Thou hast reached the camping ground:
Battles fought and victories won,
   Thou a conqueror's wreath hast found.

Death has claimed thy form alone;
   And thy spirit liveth still,
Working in diviner ways
   After God the Maker's will.

Thou hast battled for the right,
   Bravely fought and nobly fell,
Martyred in defence of truth,
   Loved by thee so long and well.

Reverent is this tribute placed
   By a loyal, stranger hand,
On this soldier's casket, one
   Called to die for native land.

Simple though its words and few,
   'Tis a tribute of the heart,
Due to one who bravely bore
   In dear Freedom's strife a part.

Soldier! rest in hallowed peace;
   Though affection's tear may fall,
Patriot hearts may yet rejoice
   That thou heardst thy country's call.

Green around thy head shall twine
   Evermore the unwithering bays;
And thy name, with freedom joined,
   Shall be whispered oft with praise.

## THE POET'S PROPHECY OF AMERICA'S FUTURE.

> "Not thine the olive, but the sword to bring;
> Not peace, but war! Yet from these shores shall spring
> Peace without end; from these with blood defiled,
> Spread the pure spirit of thy Master mild;
> Here, in his train, shall arts and arms attend, —
> Arts to adorn, and arms but to defend.
> Assembling here, all nations shall be blest;
> The sad be comforted, the weary rest;
> Untouched shall drop the the fetters of the slave;
> And he shall rule the world he died to save."
>
> *Rogers's Voyage of Columbus.*

FAR through the ages peered the poet's eye,
   The future of America to learn:
Then, with the poet's gift of prophecy,
   He showed the glory that he could discern, —
That where our striped and starry symbol shone,
True peace and freedom evermore were known.

We thank thee, Rogers! we who bear to-day
   The arms our nation's honor to defend;
Our country's natal star fades not away,
   But with the world's day dawn for aye to blend;
And when Eternity's glad sun shall rise,
Still shall our banner gleam along the skies.

Onward! still on, O hosts of freedom, press!
   The bending heavens await the final shock.
Heed not the notes of terror and distress:
   Our country rests upon Salvation's rock.
Your leader owns Immanuel for his guide,
And victory is to Christian trust allied.

Assembled here, all nations *now* are blest:
   They lend their strength our threatened land to
      save;
A few more strokes, then shall the patriot rest,
   And then "shall drop the fetters from the slave;"
While angels sing anew their Bethlehem strain,
And men, rejoicing, join the glad refrain.

---

## WAITING FOR THE HOUR.

[Suggested by W. J. Carleton's picture, entitled "Waiting for the Hour," representing slaves waiting for the time to come when the President's Emancipation Proclamation should be in force.]

THEY wait! Long, weary years have passed,
   And Liberty seemed far:
Lo! bright upon their future path
   Now beams the polar star.
God from on high his ear hath bowed,
   His the Redeemer's power:
With reverent joy and holy hope,
   They're "waiting for the hour."

That hour! the bell of Liberty
   May ring it out with joy,
When midnight stars shall sound it forth
   In the "belfries of the sky."*

---

\* Everett's Oration on "The Uses of Astronomy."

The hour of Freedom! well may he
  Who holds Time's measure there
Intently on the hour-hand gaze,
  Still " watching unto prayer."

Long had his voice proclaimed the hope
  The symbol-anchor tells; *
And yet he listens, half afraid
  To hear the chiming bells
Which tell that Freedom's hour hath dawned,
  The long, sad night is o'er,
The chains and fetters, woe and sin,
  Of slavery are no more.

Shout, friends of Liberty, aloud!
  Shout with a mighty tone!
Sing, angels in the upper world,
  A song of Freedom's own!
Now stripes and bondage are exchanged
  For peace and quiet homes,
Where no slave-driver's voice is heard,
  And never blood-hound comes.

O artist! on whose canvas glows
  This picture grand and high,
Hast thou not won by work like this
  The " Well done " of the sky?
And yet no pen can write the hopes,
  No pencil paint the joy
In all its fulness, which they knew
  To whom this hour was nigh.

---

\* The watch-key was in form of an anchor.

They wait! yet while we look, the hour
   Comes with its blissful freight:
Fling out the Stars and Stripes, a sign
   They may no longer wait.
Shout Lincoln's name with blissful tears,
   Pray for him day by day,
And, through all coming time, look back
   With joy to "Sixty-three."

## EMANCIPATION.

LAND of the Christian's hope!
   Land of the patriot's pride!
Let Freedom like a river flow, —
   A broad, deep, sparkling tide.
Break each accursed chain,
   Let the enslaved go free,
Or never hope a righteous God
   Again will prosper thee.

Earth's heathen millions wait
   For light to beam from thee:
How can it shine through that dark mist
   Of cruel slavery?
Crush the rebellion foul,
   And with it crush its cause,
The deadliest foe in all our land
   To just and humane laws.

By martyred Torrey's blood,
  By Lovejoy's honored name,
Shake off the shackles of disgrace,
  Wipe out the nation's shame:
Let not our heroes fall
  In this great strife in vain;
Nor leave it for our children dear
  To fight it o'er again.

Proclaim the edict now!
  Be tardy justice done
To those so long by us oppressed,
  And then the vict'ry's won.
God's smile will clear our sky,
  And paint the promise-bow
On each retreating cloud, to be
  The pledge of glory new.

Then speak the magic word:
  Say to the slave, "Be free!"
Let Northern bells ring in the year
  Of Southern jubilee!
Shrink not in coward fear,
  Be merciful and just,
Or look to see the Stars and Stripes
  Dishonored in the dust.

Nay, lift the dear old flag:
  More proudly let it wave
Above a nation purified,
  A people true and brave;

A North and South made one,
  In bonds that none may break,
While shouts of " Peace and Liberty ! "
  Our whole broad land awake.

---

## THE PATRIOT'S PRAYER.

WHEN drawing near the Mercy-seat, with close-shut closet-door,
And closed each avenue of thought where pressed the world before,
With rev'rence let thy spirit bend, as bend the lofty trees,
When o'er their heads sweeps strong and free the stormy autumn breeze;
Bow lower than for many a year, O man of spirit high!
And fervently with trusting heart send up this earnest cry, —
" O God! to our brave Stars and Stripes let victory be given;
'Thy kingdom come, Thy will be done, on earth as 'tis in heaven!'"

When comes the holy day of rest, and God's dear children meet
Within those walls where Jesus comes his followers oft to greet,

While songs of praise, like incense sweet, from grateful hearts ascend,
And human eloquence shall oft with heavenly wisdom blend,
Then let the patriot's earnest prayer, oft in his closet breathed,
Be echoed, and the promise claimed where many are agreed:
"O God! to our brave Stars and Stripes let victory be given;
'Thy kingdom come, Thy will be done, on earth as 'tis in heaven!'"

"Thy kingdom come!" through parted veils the truth shall then be seen,
And, as when Christ on Calvary died, the earth shall shake again;
Then thrones shall crumble, empires fall, and tyranny be o'er,
And Freedom's clarion voice proclaim Christ's reign from shore to shore;
Then shall each soul enslaved be free, and every fetter fall,
And He who gave the victory be crowned the Lord of all!
Well may we pray, "As one step forward, to us be victory given;
'Thy kingdom come, Thy will be done, on earth as 'tis in heaven!'"

"Thy will be done!" Oh! when, indeed, thy law is here obeyed,
Before the righteous rulers shall the evil be afraid;

Then fraud and falsehood, demons dread, their sable
  wings shall fold,
And not a Judas sell this land for silver or for gold;
Then 'neath his vine and fig-tree the patriot saint
  shall dwell,
And praise that guiding Providence "who doeth all
  things well,"
And sing with voice melodious, like that to seraphs
  given,
"'Thy kingdom come, Thy will be done, on earth as
  'tis in heaven!'"

## THE LAWRENCE MASSACRE.

OH, sight of horror! lo, the midnight stars
    Grow dim, as war's smoke slowly upward
      goes, —
Not smoke of warfare waged in Honor's sight,
    But unprovoked assault on unarmed foes.

The loyal friends of Freedom calmly rest
    One moment on the pillow won by toil;
Then, roused by shouts, half-wakened, meet the foe,
    Only to sleep again on Kansas soil,

Sleep the long sleep that knows no troubled dream,
    Martyrs for Freedom! long to be revered,
Whose name shall shine on our historic page,
    To whom heart-monuments shall yet be reared.

Go, look upon that scene, by artist hand
    Now pencilled on the glowing canvas there,
Then vow, like ancient hero, ne'er to faint
    Till triumph gilds that hour of black despair.

Till martyr blood again the seed shall prove
    Of Liberty through all our suffering land,
And Peace with grateful joy again is hailed
    By all the States, a free and loyal band.

## WHERE IS HE?

[A mother, whose son has fallen in defence of our beloved country, thus wrote to me: "The lines by ———, I should like them *so* much. Can I obtain them through you? When I watched his baby face with streaming tears, painting sad pictures in the far off yet to be, I little thought how alleviating such precious gifts, in actual sorrow and suffering, would be. I gather them up to fill the vacancy. Even the touching letters of some of his comrades, so full of soul, I hug to my heart. Still, *you* know, the mother, in a moment of anguish, will ask of all the world, '*Where is he?*'" Her words have suggested the following stanzas:] —

THEY say that his body is laid in the grave;
    They say for his country he died;
But the mother-heart in its loneliness throbs,
    And has still in its anguish sighed,
"Oh! where is he now, — my generous boy!
    My precious one! where is he?
Will he never return, in the battle who fell
    As he fought 'neath the flag of the free?

Where is he? I tended his baby form;
    I watched him in childhood's glee;
I cheered his young manhood, and hoped his strength
    Would be prop in old age for me.
But I gave him up when his country called;
    I laid him on Freedom's shrine:
Oh! why should I murmur if God, who asked
    For the offering, accepted mine?

I murmur not, though the far-off West
    Is the grave for such as he,
While I must miss him forevermore
    From my home by the sounding sea:
For my country needs in this peril-hour
    The costliest gifts, I know;
Then I'll murmur not, but I still must weep.
    I'm his mother, and loved him so!

I am cheered by the shout of the victor-host;
    I rejoice in the triumph of Right;
And I look on the flag with a loving eye
    Beneath which my son could fight;
And the comforting words which pitying friends
    Are speaking so oft to me, —
They are welcome, — I'm thankful; but, midst them all,
    I whisper, "Where is he?"

His merry laugh and his graceful form,
    His words full of kindness and love,
Shall I know them no more, save by Memory's power,
    Till I meet my young soldier above?

I will try to be patient, O land of my birth!
    I'm willing to suffer for thee ;
And the patriot's fire in my heart still burns,
    Though I'm asking " Where is he ? "

O God of the mother whose holy trust
    Is placed on thy promise sure !
Give strength to the torn and bleeding hearts
    Counted worthy to endure,
And answer the cry, "Oh ! where is he ? "
    With the whisper to each sad heart,
" Though he comes no more, thou shalt go to him :
    Ye shall meet no more to part."

## THE SOLDIER AND THE TEACHER.

[Suggested by the funerals of Sergeant Charles F. Ferguson and Miss Rebecca F. Prince.]

OUR martyred dead!
    They speak to us from many a grave,
Far off or near, — they who would save
Our country in her hour of pain,
And find in loss eternal gain ;
Whose fresh young lives were laid too soon
Upon the altar, ere Life's noon
Had scarcely come, and while each heart
Throbbed wildly comfort to impart
To this fair land, all stricken now,
And made beneath the rod to bow.

Our God, who "doeth all things well,"
Hath given us the flag-decked bier,
The muffled drum, the falling tear,
And, harsh and sharp, the funeral-bell,
Instead of merry shout and song,
As victor armies marched along,
And broken circles were made whole,
  While parted friends clasped hands again :
Ah me ! to greet their patriot dead
  How many fond hearts wait in vain !

    The patriot host
Go not alone into the halls,
  The "silent halls of death : "
From quiet homes and peaceful haunts
Goes up the parting breath ;
And one who loved her Master well,
And of his dying love would tell
To pupils dear, and sing his praise
On glad, returning sabbath days,
Hath ceased her labors here below,
And soared where sister-seraphs glow,
And, with a sweet and pure renown,
Hath taken Life's immortal crown.
Young eyes were dimmed with tears for her
  Who taught them day by day,
That she no more with them, on earth,
  Would tread in wisdom's way ;
And many a parent's heart grew sad,
As children wept o'er teacher dead.
For her the white robe well might be
  The garland, and the cross

Of beauteous emblem-blossoms sweet, —
　　Since ours alone the loss.

　　　Years will roll on.
The soldier in his honored tomb
　　Will hear no noise of war;
The teacher in her quiet grave
　　Will know no schoolroom jar;
And on the hearts which loved them her
　　Their names inscribed shall be,
Till every heart hath tasted death,
　　And death no more shall see.

　　　Look up and on!
The light that shines afar comes down
　　From heaven's pearly gate,
And none who knock in Jesus' name
　　Outside shall ever wait.
Behold the dawning of that day,
　　The coming of that hour,
When all our griefs shall pass away,
　　And sin shall lose its power!
Far up the heavenly heights I see
　　"The Lamb for sinners slain."
Fear not, O mourning heart! for thee
　　The dead shall live again.
Washed in the fountain of thy blood,
　　O Saviour! all shall be
Who in thy might each foe withstood,
　　And humbly looked to thee.
He in thy realm of peace shall rest
　　Who in thy name hath fought,
And by the Master's side shall dwell
　　The teacher and the taught.

Farewell to both!
Soldier and teacher, rest!
Room is there for you in the leaf-clad earth,
Room on the Saviour's breast!

## THE DEAD SOLDIER.

THEY had smoothed his limbs for the last, long sleep;
That graceful form was still;
And the clustering curls on his forehead slept
Like flowers which the dew-drops fill.

But oh! on his face was a heavenly smile,
A look which the angels wear,
As if he had drank from the cup of joy,
And his heart was free from care.

A smile that told of an angel guard
By the form of the soldier dead,—
Aye, told yet more, that the light of heaven
Around that form was shed;

That the soul, as it sped to the realms of bliss,
Went forth with exultant joy:
Accept the omen, O mother-heart
That weeps for thy soldier-boy!

He may not tread in the paths he loved
With the voice and smile of yore;
But his spirit may still commune with thine
As he looks from the "shining shore."

And his voice to thee, like his parting smile,
   Is the echo of hope and joy;
Saying, "Faint not till thy work is done,
   Then come to thy darling boy!"

So gird thee, mother, for future strife;
   Toil on in the path assigned
By the Infinite Wisdom that looks to see
   Thy will to his resigned.

And the hour shall come, when, the dark veil rent,
   Thy soul shall be filled with joy,
As amid the crowned, victorious host,
   Thou shalt greet thy patriot boy.

---

## JUBILEE GUNS.

[Written in Reading, Mass., on hearing the salute ordered by Gov. Andrew on New-Year's Day, 1866.]

THE cannons peal, twelve miles away:
   Rejoice, O Freedom's sons!
Old Massachusetts hails to-day
   The thunder of those guns.

Ring out the bells! Ring Liberty
   O'er all our land afar, —
The fruit of weary years of toil,
   The guerdon of the war!

We look, through blinding tears perchance,
  Upon our flag so fair;
Yet on the bended knee give thanks
  That still it waveth there, —

That still it waves, the symbol high
  Of freedom to the world,
Of liberty to every soul
  Where'er it is unfurled.

Then let the joy-bells loudly ring,
  The deep-mouthed cannons roar:
Our nation can the challenge fling
  She never flung before.

Tremble, O earth! beneath the jar
  Of Freedom's guns to-day;
Yet shrink not; for the sounds of war,
  Thank God! have died away.

These tell of broken chains, and hearts
  With joy almost oppressed,
As slavery for aye departs,
  And fugitives find rest.

Oh, 'tis a glorious thing to live
  In this rejoicing time, —
This blessed year of jubilee, —
  'Tis joyful and sublime!

Lord, let thy servants now depart:
  Their eyes salvation see.
This rescued land is Freedom's own;
  Thine shall the glory be.

## THE MOTHERS OF THE BRAVE.

ON many a breezy height,
   In many a bosky dell,
And on the broad, green prairie land,
   They lie who bravely fell,
The champions of Liberty,
Fighting, O land we love! for thee.

In many a far-off home,
   Beside the lonely hearth,
Fond mothers sit, and think of those
   To whom they once gave birth,
Now born into a higher life,
Amid the din of Freedom's strife.

O mothers of the brave!
   Whose sons have won renown,
Weep not that they so soon exchanged
   Earth for a hero's crown:
Now patriot laurels, nobly won,
Enwreath the brow of each dear son.

And ye who trust in Him
   Who saveth evermore,
Hope still to meet those hero sons
   Upon a brighter shore:
No war shall scourge that better land,
No sin need God's corrective hand.

When Peace illumes our land,
   And Freedom's blessed light
Gleams even from the humblest cot,
   Your pathway shall be bright,
Who once your household jewels gave,
O honored mothers of the brave!

---

## THE DESTRUCTION OF THE MERRIMAC.

HA! sound the clashing cymbals! blow loud a trumpet blast!
Let clarion notes re-echo the tidings far and fast!
Lo! fallen on the field of strife the giant that defied
Our little David when he came with stones from streamlet's side.
Smote was he on that sabbath morn when gallant Worden fought,
Now stripped of weapons, armor, all, his head in triumph brought.

As Salem's maidens calmly viewed Goliath's harmless head,
So to the bowers of ladies fair the Merrimac is sped, —
The blackened ruins, chip by chip, are borne across the land;
And gentle spirits bless the Power that gave it to each hand.
For, hearken! have you heart the tale? (it is unfolded far,)
*No more* the Merrimac defies our little Monitor.

Forsaken! burned! exploded! then was strewn the waters dark
With remnants of the shattered, aye, ruined rebel barque;
And thus, ere long, shall perish the vile confederate host,—
Melt like the dew of morning, and be forever lost;
Each man, reluctantly compelled to serve the rebel cause,
When Union forces break his chains, trampling the flag of bars,
And traitors find in flight or fight their only, last resource,
Save when they take the Merrimac's own suicidal course.
Yes! bid triumphal music wake the echoes far and wide;
For the charred, misshapen fragments upon the James's tide
Alone can show the Merrimac, that terror of the hour,
When iron-clad vessels over wood displayed their fearful power.
Revenged are ye who at your post, the Cumberland, went down;
Revenged, ye of the Congress whose death hath won renown;
Revenged! for in her suicide she hath confessed her wrong.*
Like justice shall be meted yet to all the rebel throng.

May 13, 1862.

* "Suicide is confession."— Daniel Webster.

## "IT IS WELL."

[When the Rev. George Trask heard of the death of his son Josiah (the worthy and talented editor of "The Kansas State Gazette"), who was among the victims of the Kansas Massacre, he gently responded, "It is well!" and went immediately to his own room, where he remained for some time, and then came forth with the serenity of a Christian who truly believes that his God and Father "doeth all things well."]

"IT is well!" he hath died for the country he loved,
    Though he died not 'mid war's din and rattle:
Not alone are they heroes for Freedom who fight,
    And then fall on the red field of battle:
Unarmed as was Christ, with the soul of a Tell,
He hath fallen for Freedom! My country! "'tis
    well!"

"It is well!" he hath lifted the standard full oft
    Around which true spirits might rally,
And sounded the tocsin of war for the Right,
    In Kansas o'er mountain and valley:
By voice and by pen he rang Liberty's bell, —
He hath fallen for Freedom! Great West! "It is
    well!"

"It is well!" he hath gone in his manhood's fair
    prime,
    While brightly his future was dawning;
But oh! we will hope that an angel was Death
    To show him the gleam of life's morning!
Then hush vain regrets in each bosom that swell,
He hath fallen for Freedom! O God! "it is well!"

Though darkened the home of his loved ones to-day;
  Though tears dim their eyes, love attesting;
And heavy the stroke upon one widowed heart, —
  On God are they all sweetly resting.
With the ransomed our country's brave martyrs shall
    dwell:
*He* hath fallen for Freedom! Our Father! " 'tis
  well!"

## THE YOUNG SOLDIER.

[A tribute to the memory of the late HERVEY DIX of Malden, who was killed while fighting bravely against great odds, in a skirmish, near Kirksville, Mo., August, 1861.]

HE sleeps afar from friends and home,
  New England's son so brave!
Kind stranger hands his form prepared
  To fill an honored grave.

He lived not long enough to gain
  Scott's world-wide martial fame,
But, dying, rose to Ellsworth's side,
  And won a hero's name.

Bright shall the everlasting bays
  Around his young head twine;
And Liberty's dear lovers make
  His grave the patriot's shrine.

O fond maternal heart! that bled,
   When o'er the quivering wire,
With sudden shock, the tidings came,
   That he had "gone up higher."

Thou mother of a hero son!
   Smile through thy falling tears,
Till Hope's bright rainbow gilds the path
   Thou'lt tread in coming years.

When Peace shall bless our struggling land,
   And Freedom's battle's won,
Thy mourning heart, with Christian faith
   Will throb, "Thy will be done."

And when Life's evening shadows steal
   Across thy dying eye,
Lo! waiting for thy greetings fond
   Will be thy hero boy.

## LIBERTY TO ALL.

HOTTER grows the fiery furnace,
   Higher rise the flames,
Faster on the list of glory
   Throng the immortal names:
What shall be the end at last,
When the war is over-past?

Tears like summer showers are falling,
   Crushing summer blooms;
Human hearts are daily bleeding
   In a thousand homes:
What shall be the glory gained,
What the glad result attained?

Freedom is the blessed burden
   Of each weary year;
And the birth-throes of her glory
   Are the groans we hear:
God will give his people rest
When with freedom all are blest!

---

## A PRAYER FOR ABRAHAM LINCOLN.

GOD of our fathers! Thou whose hand
   Thine ancient people led,
Look down on our beloved land,
   And bless our nation's head.
Oh give him wisdom, Lord, to guide
   The hosts of freedom now, —
To meet the ills which may betide
   With calm, unruffled brow!

We pray that he in peace may rule
   O'er this broad, favored land,
No craven heart! no party's tool!
   But with a righteous hand;

And o'er our land, from east to west,
   From north to south, proclaim
(Obeying duty's high behest)
   The Union's honored name.

Sustain him by thy might, O God!
   In every trying scene,
In judgment hall, on fields of blood,
   Or in his home serene.
Oh nerve his arm to strike each blow
   At treason and at wrong,
And bid him triumph o'er each foe,
   And sing the victor's song!

God of our fathers! bless this man,
   The people's only choice,
And guide him with thine own right hand,
   And by thy Spirit's voice.
And when on History's page his name
   In future years is seen,
May unborn millions guard his fame,
   And bless thee for his reign!

Hear thou our prayer, and in thy way,
   And in thine own best time,
Deliver us from Slavery's sway,
   And ring out Freedom's chime.
Bless him now at our nation's helm,
   O Lord! we pray again;
And let no waves his bark o'erwhelm,
   For Jesus' sake — Amen.

## THE WHITE HYACINTH FROM HAMPTON.*

"BEAUTY for ashes!" when the patriot true
    Trod streets deserted by their wonted feet,
And gazed upon the blackened ruins there, —
    The work of rebels ere their swift retreat,
Amid the ashes of that town so doomed,
He saw rare beauty from the Father's hand,
As the pale Hyacinth looked up and smiled,
    Like patient sufferer in a down-trod land.

"Beauty for ashes!" — blooming 'mid the wreck
    Of cherished hearth-stones and beloved haunts,
Type of the glorious blossom yet to grow
    And flourish here, in spite of traitor vaunts.
Slavery shall die, and Liberty survive,
    As God shall live while earthly thrones decay.
Praise God, my soul! the Builder still hath power
    To raise the structure vandals low would lay.

"Beauty for ashes!" Type of childhood's games,
    Thou hyacinth from Hampton's ash-strewn streets,
Type also of the worse than childish course
    Pursued by those who burn, as they retreat,
The homes of true hearts and the haunts of those
    Who loved the flag which tells of liberty.
Oh, worse than folly! for a Judas-doom
    Awaits the rebel foemen of the free.

* Suggested by receiving a flower gathered by Rev. Arthur B. Fuller, Chaplain Sixteenth Massachusetts Volunteers, from amid the ruins and desolation of Hampton, after the rebels had fled, leaving the town in ashes.

"Beauty for ashes!" let the pæans sound!
   The ruined towns along the path of war,
The desolation of Rebellion's land,
   Tell to the lookers-on from homes afar,
That suff'ring follows sin; and, as the flower
   Looked up and smiled amid the whelming gloom,
So looks the patriot, with faith in Right,
   Peace to behold where Freedom's hosts may come

"Beauty for ashes!" as the chains shall fall
   From long-crushed millions in our guilty land,
So victory cometh to our arms again,
   And peace, affrighted dove, will soon descend;
Then with perennial loveliness shall bloom
   The flower of liberty, whose fragrance sweet,
As the magnolia of the sunny South,
   Or Northern violet, all mankind shall greet.
     1862.

## THE BURIED VOLUNTEER.

NOT where his fathers rest, beside the sea,
   But far away upon Potomac's shore,
Or in the distant West, his grave may be,
   Who comes to his New-England home no more.

Fond hearts are aching in their silent grief,
   Within the cot which love a palace made;
While patriot pride and Christian hope relief
   Offers to those who mourn their cherished dead.

Comfort will come, but only, Lord, from thee.
   In thee, O Christ! alone the heart is glad,
Whose earthly hopes like shadows seem to flee,
   Whose loss uncounted makes each moment sad.

When to the din of battle he, the brave,
   Rushed like a hero, at his country's call,
He thought to win a garland or the grave,
   To live a conqueror, or a martyr fall.

Now angels chant their pæans o'er his head;
   The land he loved, the land for which he died,
Counts him amid her dear and honored dead,
   And writes his name on History's page with pride.

O buried volunteer! thy praise shall sound
   Sweet in thy children's ears in days to be;
And, when blest freedom circles earth around,
   God, with truth's champions, will remember thee.

APRIL 4, 1862.

## A PRAYER FOR THE UNION.

*"Liberty and Union, now and forever, one and inseparable."*
                              DANIEL WEBSTER.

IN this dark hour of national dismay,
   O God of liberty, thy power display!
Thine hand in safety led thine ancient band,
Through paths of danger, to their promised land.

Thine arm defended those who bravely bore
The rights of freemen to this western shore,
Who dared the whelming wave and tempest's shock,
To plant a freeman's foot on Plymouth Rock;
And when oppression from Old England came,
And brightly blazed anew the holy flame
Of liberty, each noble heart the shrine,
Thou ledst them on to victory, Power Divine!
God guided pens that wrote the nation's will;
God led the hosts who fought on Bunker's Hill:
So, Lord, now treason in our land is rife,
Appear for our deliverance, end the strife,
And let the "ides of March," in sixty-one,
See Lincoln prove a second Washington,
Through thee our nation saving from a fall,
The wild waves quelling ere they whelm us all,
Till over our broad land, from shore to shore,
Blend Liberty and Union evermore.

## A FLOWER FROM A REBEL'S GRAVE.

[Suggested by a flower gathered by Rev. Arthur B. Fuller, and given to the writer by the lamented chaplain, May 16, 1862.]

BRIGHT floweret from a lowly spot
    Where rests a son of earth,
Thou speakest trumpet-toned to me
    Of thy far place of birth,
And of my enemy who rests
Where blossoms smile o'er manly breasts.

That land! by slavery accursed,
   Now Freedom's blood-stained ground,
Henceforth within its borders shall
   The free alone be found.
O God of battles! thanks to thee
Who victory gave to Liberty.

That grave! My enemy lies there;
   And thus shall yet lie low
The hydra-headed treason which
   Made him my country's foe:
Thus may each rebel soldier lie,
If only thus may treason die.

My enemy! alas, that thou
   Should'st die in such a cause!
Rebelling 'gainst the truth, the right,
   In government and laws.
I will not say thou wast not brave,
But thine is not an honored grave.

My heart is sad for those who weep
   Within thy Southern home,
Since thou to greet them canst no more
   With rapid footsteps come:
I pity every loving heart
Which feels the sting of sorrow's dart.

Yet, blossom from a rebel's grave!
   With golden hue so fair,
I would that he had nobler lived
   Who silent sleepeth there.
So lived that he in death could claim
A loyal hero's honored name.

No laurel wreath I'd twine for him
    Whose fratricidal hand
Was raised to scatter blight and death
    Far o'er our favored land.
Thank God! his power for ill is o'er;
So perish traitors evermore.

## THE SIEGE OF CHARLESTON.

[Suggested by a scene in Perham's "Mirror of the Rebellion."]

DOOMED city! Treason's nest should be destroyed!
    Thou dost thy doom deserve.
On, in the name of Liberty and God,
    Ye who would still preserve
The glorious flag with stripes all whole and bright,
Each star reflecting Liberty's own light.

Slowly but surely are thy stones removed;
    Thy pride at last must fall:
How with foundation gone can longer stand
    Rebellion's tottering wall?
Charleston! Palmyra's ruins symbolized
Thy fate, O ingrate! sadly now unwise.

The slumbering form of Calhoun cannot save
    Thine honor from the dust:
Like thee must fall at last, in dread dismay,
    All who have placed their trust

Upon the quicksands of Rebellion's cause,
And spurn alike our liberties and laws.

Brave band of heroes Sumter gathering round,
    Be fearless and press on!
Soon must the day of glad success to you
    In blissful radiance dawn.
Our flag must wave in every State again,
And Peace and Freedom o'er us gently reign.

---

## THE UNION ARMY NEVER SURRENDERS.

[One who fell in defence of our country in the early days of the rebellion said when his little band were called upon to surrender to five times the same number of rebels, that those belonging to his regiment *never* surrendered. His brave and memorable words echo the sentiment of the Union army, and have suggested the following lines: —]

SURRENDER? Nay! though thick around
    Death-dealing shot may fly,
While clouds of sulphurous smoke obscure
    The calm o'er-arching sky.
Loud let our cannon thunder forth
    Defiance to the foe,
And with the gleaming bayonet
    Our soldiers onward go!

What though our serried ranks are thinned,
    Or mowed like summer grass,
And on they press, outnumbering us,
    A huge, o'erwhelming mass?

Yet we will stand the sudden shock,
   Resisting till in vain,
And only slowly backward move,
   To " bide our time " again.

From brave hearts on Potomac's shore,
   Or in the distant West,
Or 'mid the hills of Tennessee,
   Or where the surging crest
Of many a wave sweeps noble barks
   That bear our flag on high,
Comes, ever and anon, the shout,
   " We conquer or we die ! "

Surrender !  Give our broad, free lands
   To dark Rebellion's sway ?
Hark ! every breeze from out the North
   Bears back the answer, " Nay ! "
And gentle woman stronger feels,
   And children happier grow,
As, leaning on a Mighty Arm,
   Our Union answers " No ! "

Then fill the broken ranks again,
   And hasten to the strife ;
Aye ! in the holiest war e'er waged,
   Press on to peril life.
Our starry banner yet shall float
   Upon the ambient air,
While deep-mouthed guns our cause proclaim
   Triumphant everywhere.

## "ALL QUIET ALONG THE POTOMAC."

[Suggested by a photograph with that title.]

All quiet along the river now,
   And winter reigneth there.
The ground is carpeted with snow,
   And chill the evening air.
Above the snow-clad earth arise
   The stones which mark the spots
Where rest the forms of those we prize,
   Our martyred patriots.

On yonder highland stands to-night
   The sentinel alone,
His musket gleaming in the light
   Of the pale winter moon.
How oft to him at midnight hour,
   Above the noble dead,
Doth Memory come with magic power
   To speak of those who bled, —

Who fought in Freedom's sacred cause,
   Beneath our banner bright, —
The symbol each true heart adores, —
   The emblem of the right, —
And fell before the rebel host,
   But won a pure renown,
Whose lustre never shall be lost,
   A patriot martyr's crown!

"All quiet upon Potomac's shore!"
   Soft may the river glide!
Life, with its conflicts, now is o'er
   For heroes by its side.
But far on high, where never comes
   The sound of ruthless war,
Those patriots found the saint's sweet home,
   And meet with foes no more.

Each wild alarm, each whistling ball,
   Each shrieking shell, is gone:
Henceforth their anthems rise and fall
   Where gleams celestial morn.
And while upon the lonely shore
   Their honored dust may rest,
Each Christian patriot evermore
   With victory is blest.

## FREEDOM IN POLAND.

NOW, God be praised! the fetters fast are falling,
   The voice of Freedom sounds in lands afar:
Above the clouds of war, my soul appalling,
   I see the shining of the Bethlehem star.

Poland has freedom! God alone hath done it:
   The hearts of kings are in his hand alone;
No strife of arms, no pleading voice, hath won it:
   Take thou the praise, O Lord! it is thine own.

The Sobieskies smile from heights of glory;
    Brave Kosciusko shouts with holy joy.
I see them cast their crowns, O Lord! before thee,
    Amid the host of Freedom's sons on high.

Long may the Polish peasant, freedom sharing,
    Clasp hands with us across the mighty sea;
Love the good Czar, in God's own time appearing
    To do his will, but give the praise to Thee!

For thou alone hast freed them, mighty Leader!
    Stretch thou thine arm above *our* crimson sea!
Let Poland see that the same God who freed her
    Hath given us peace, and made our bondmen free!

# MEMORIAL POEMS.

# MEMORIAL POEMS.

## THE RIGHTEOUS SHALL BE HAD IN EVERLASTING REMEMBRANCE.

### TO MRS. A. A. F.

ONCE more I lay Love's offering on thy grave,
    Dear friend and true!
With longing heart thine unforgotten smile
    Once more to view.

How ached our torn hearts as we laid thee down
    Upon that autumn day,
When all the brightness of that hour was dimmed,
    For thou hadst passed away!

All through the weary months that followed on,
    Still have we mourned
Our loss in thy departure, friend beloved!
    Now glory-crowned.

But oft sweet whispers to our spirits come
    From that bright shore
Where thou art resting, and we hope anew
    To greet once more.

Sweet friend! we'll cherish in our heart of hearts
        Thy virtues rare,
And pray that in thy meek, quiet, gentle ways,
        We all may share.

And that the mantle of thy spirit rest
        On those who tread,
Humbly and rev'rently, where thou didst walk
        In years now fled.

Rest, precious dust! in consecrated ground.
        The soul hath soared
We know, and through those weary, vanished months
        Hath God adored,

Where angels bow with harps to love attuned,
        And souls like thine
Grow beauteous in Love's light, yet more and more
        And more divine.

But the dear lips our love once gladly pressed
        Lie buried here;
The hand that clasped our own in friendship's grasp,
        The soft, dark hair.

And o'er this grave we must in sadness bend,
        Till our turn come
To reach that land where tombstones never rise, —
        Thy new, bright home.

# FIRST TIME. — LAST TIME. — NEXT TIME.

#### INSCRIBED TO THE MEMORY OF MRS. A. A. F.

THE stars were shining in the evening sky,
   As I, a stranger, entered at her door.
She welcomed me with smile so full of peace
   I trusted her sweet spirit from that hour.
My hand I gave her in unfaltering faith
That she would be my friend in life and death.

I scarce knew why; but ever from that hour,
   When *first* I saw her placid face, I grew
To love her smile, her voice, her pleasant ways,
   Until she was a friend no longer new:
And, clinging to her like a weary child,
I sighed to be like her, the pure and mild.

*Last time* I looked upon that face so dear,
   'Twas marble-like in coldness, pale and still:
No answering look the closed eyes gave to cheer,
   There was no smile my loving heart to thrill.
Within the coffin, flower-decked, still she lay, —
The form, I mean, — the soul had passed away.

Which was the *last time?* When her eyes met mine
   That sabbath morn, and smiled her love once more,
Ere the death-angel, sent by love divine,
   Bore her freed spirit to the shining shore;
Or when I stood her open grave beside,
And smoothed the dark locks of my pastor's bride?

*Next time*, — thank God! there is a glad *next* time,
   When I shall look upon my friend again, —
Shall see her radiant 'mid the white-robed throng,
   And hear her voice in some sublime refrain.
She ever loved to sing the songs of Zion:
She sings them now where reigneth Judah's Lion.

Next time, and not far off that blessed hour,
   My hand shall gently touch her noble brow:
She'll greet me with her own sweet voice and smile.
   How thrills my heart with that glad prospect now!
Pass on, ye seasons! bring the summer hour,
When I shall greet her in some heavenly bower.

## ONLY OUT OF SIGHT.

**TO MRS. ABBY A. FOSTER.**

DEAR friend, thou'rt only out of sight, —
   Sweet sister of my soul!
One little stream alone doth now
   Between our spirits roll;
One step, — the last, — and I shall greet
   Thy cherished smile again;
One pang, — the last, — and I shall know
   Again no parting pain.

Unfading as these evergreens
   Thy memory shall be;
Unwithering as these amaranths
   Our loving thoughts of thee.

Sweet sister! cherished friend! with tears
  I place them here to-day:
Thy grave is hallowed ground to me,
  Where I may weep and pray.


Oft, in my distant home, I sit,
  And live that sabbath o'er,
When by thy side I stood, till thou
  Crossed to the shining shore.
And evermore both " bright and fair "
  As thine my hope shall be;
For in thy footsteps will I tread,
  Safe while I follow thee.


Christ was thy light, thy guide, thy hope;
  And thou art with him now,
The palm of victory in thine hand,
  The crown upon thy brow.
Yet often art thou still with us;
  Thy spirit o'er us bends;
And sweetly dost thou minister
  To thine earth-fettered friends.


I hear thy voice at midnight hour,
  I hear it oft at noon:
Thou smilest with the morning star,
  And with the calm, bright moon.
I never can forget thee — no!
  To thee henceforth is given
To blend with all my thoughts of death,
  And all my hopes of heaven.

Soon shall we clasp the friendly hand
  In those unfading bowers,
Where, as on earth, thou'lt pluck for me
  Some earliest, sweetest flowers;
And I shall find our love's strong chain
  By death was unclasped never,
Where all we love shall live again,
  And part no more forever.

Nov. 2, 1864.

## IN MEMORY OF MRS. E. A. TENNEY.

We sit, with mourning hearts, beneath the shadow
  Which darkens now our home,
And look with longing eyes to that bright region
  Where shadows never come.

We think of her, now from our side departed,
  In Christian hope and trust:
Gentle and lovely, pure and earnest-hearted,
  She dwells among the just.

Through summer's long, bright days she lingered with us;
  Then, with the falling leaf,
She faded from our sight, and heaven's garner
  Received a ripened sheaf.

Love watched unceasingly beside her pillow;
  And prayer went up on high,
That she might ride triumphant o'er death's billow,
  When beckoned to the sky.

We look to Thee, who hast in wisdom taken
  That which thy love hath given :
Our faith in thy dear love shall be unshaken,
  Till we meet her in heaven.

Bless Thou the husband from his chosen severed ;
  Guide Thou their darling's feet ;
And in the Christian's long and blest hereafter
  Give them again to meet.

Oh ! soothe each heart by this bereavement stricken, —
  The brothers, sisters, here,
And that dear brother for our country toiling,
  A patriot young and dear.

We leave our prayer with Thee, O gentle Saviour !
  Who once wept by a grave :
Come as the Comforter to all our spirits,
  And point us o'er the wave !

---

## TO A. A. F.

THE summer skies above me bend ;
  Round me June's roses blow :
Where art thou wandering, O my friend ?
  What paths do thy feet know ?

I may not tell: to mortal eye
    The vision is not given.
Thy footsteps sound above the sky,
    Thy pathways are in heaven.

While other eyes, with tender love,
    Are gazing into mine,
What eyes among the blest above
    Are looking into thine?
While other voices fill my ear,
    Unknown, dear friend, to thee,
What music utterance dost thou hear
    Whose echoes reach not me?

I hear no answer from on high;
    Thy voice I hear no more.
But soon myself, above the sky
    And on the shining shore,
I shall discover all I ask;
    I need no answer here:
And thine shall be the joyful task
    To teach me, sister dear.

And I shall see the friends that now
    In thy dear presence throng:
With heaven's laurel round my brow,
    I'll join thy grateful song.
And, till that glorious hour shall come,
    In duty's path I'll tread,—
The path that to thy heavenly home,
    To thee, my friend, shall lead.

The summer hours will swiftly glide
   To meet the autumnal sea;
And I upon their gentle tide
   Am drawing nearer thee, —
Yes, nearer to thy side, sweet friend,
   Where I can clasp thy hand,
And love's eternal years shall spend
   In that bright, happy land.

---

## THE ASCENDED SAINT.

[Suggested by the recent death of Mrs. Margaret Fuller, the honored mother of the late Margaret, Countess d'Ossoli, of Rev. Arthur B. Fuller, and R. F. Fuller, Esq., of Boston. Her daughter, Ellen Kilshaw Channing, and her son, Eugene Fuller, Esq., have both recently departed this life; the latter by drowning, like his sister Margaret.]

SOFTLY the sunset of the sabbath passed,
   The western glory faded into night;
And, with the parting hours of holy time,
   A Christian spirit took its upward flight.

Her years on earth were many, and those years
   All filled with usefulness and holy love:
Sorrow had disciplined her soul for heaven,
   And trials fitted her for rest above.

Shall we in sackcloth mourn when such depart,
   Free spirits, like fair, uncaged birds, **to soar**
Far up and on toward wisdom infinite,
   'Mid glories mortal minds may not explore?

Oh, no! we'll lift on high a triumph song:
   For, *jubilate!* all her griefs are o'er.
Loved ones are left, but oh! she greeteth now
   The loved and wept-for who had gone before.

Death hath removed each dark veil from her eye,
   And radiant spirits walk with her in white:
No sea in heaven shrouds beloved forms,
   No sorrow there, no weary, gloomy night.

Strike, strike your harps! sing loud, ye angel choir,
   And welcome gladly this companion new, —
New in the courts of heaven, youth-renewed,
   But long ago, it may be, known to you.

The saint, ascending to his own "sweet home,"
   Claims from no sorrowing hearts a tear or sigh:
We mourn for those who tread earth's pathway still,
   But not for saints triumphant called to die.

Peace to the weary dust whose pain is o'er!
   Joy to the spirit whose long race is run!
God comfort those who wait the summons home,
   Hoping to meet her when their work is done!
1859.

---

## MARGARET FULLER OSSOLI.

FRIEND of humanity! whose warm, true heart
   Throbbed ever to redeem a fallen race,
Alas! that thou from earthly scenes shouldst part,
   Ere thou hadst reached in joy thy native place.

Thy noble husband, too, whose manly soul
   Longed for fair freedom in *his* native land,
Alas! that ocean's waves o'er him should roll,
   Ere he could view in peace Columbia's strand.

And that sweet "bird of promise," whose fair bloom,
   Evoked from out thy paradise of love,
Once made so fragrant thine Italian home, —
   He, too, went with thee to the land above.

An undivided circle! nevermore
   Will tears of sad farewell your cheeks bedew;
For on that other, that celestial shore,
   Our God unites for aye pure hearts and true.

Margaret! thy name hath long been to my soul
   A talisman of influence pure and strong;
Though born a woman, born to have control
   O'er human hearts for virtue far and long.

Thy name shall be remembered when shall die
   The name of many a warrior of renown;
For thou on nobler fields won victory,
   And gained from history a glorious crown.

Oh for the day when Italy shall know
   How to be truly free, in virtue strong!
We wonder not that thou didst love her so, —
   Home of the classics and the land of song!

When dawns that day on fair Italia's shore,
   Thou shalt be well remembered by the free:
America and Europe evermore
   Shall, as the friend of Freedom, think of thee.

And happier thought! where souls, from every chain
  Made free, forever sing redeeming grace,
There shall thy loved ones hear thy voice again,
  And look with deepest joy upon thy face.

They who love man love God; and they who toil
  To break the chains from men and minds below
Win, through the Lamb, a right to heaven's soil,
  Where boundless progress each glad soul may
    know.

God make me worthy, Margaret, to meet thee,
  And list to thy rich converse on the shore
Where holy love from heart to heart flows free,
  And weary spirits rest forevermore.

---

## REV. ARTHUR BUCKMINSTER FULLER.*

BORNE o'er death's rolling wave on angel
    pinions,
      Our brother rests
Where blessed Peace rules all the fair dominions,
      And war's rude crests,
And martial notes, and hosts arrayed for battle,
      Are known no more;
And never swords shall clash, nor death-balls rattle,
      Upon that shore.

* Chaplain Sixteenth Massachusetts, killed at Fredericksburg.

A hero, in the strife for Freedom dying.
        Immortal bays
Shall deck the brow in Death's embrace now lying;
        And tuneful lays
From hearts sincere his virtues be declaring
        Who gave his all,—
Home, health and life,—obedient on hearing
        His country's call.

Yet sad our hearts who mourn the friend so cherished,
        The noble soul,
Thank God! who lives, while but our hopes have perished,
        And at the goal
Of our short race will bid us welcome gladly;
        And each true heart
Forget the pangs which here it feels so sadly,
        While friends depart.

O brother! 'neath the shadow we shall wander,
        And think of thee:
Upon thy many virtues sweetly ponder,
        And pray to be
Where thou art resting on the shores immortal,
        With those so dear
Who earlier entered heaven's gleaming portal,
        And left thee here.

Thou faithful servant of the High and Holy!
        Heaven shall be
Still nearer to the souls, that, bending lowly,
        Now mourn for thee,

And, with the Everlasting Arm beneath them,
    Float with the tide
Which bears them on where thou ere long shall greet them,
    The other side.

Hero and saint! enrolled upon the pages
    Of history,
Telling of deeds sublime to future ages,
    Thy name shall be.
And, better still, the Lamb's resplendent volume
    Thy name shall bear,
Heading, perchance, a long and brilliant column
    Of heroes there.

Farewell for time! no more we here shall greet thee;
    But far on high,
Amid the angels, we shall surely meet thee,
    No more to die.
And from our lips the chalice, now so bitter,
    Our God will take,
And bid us drink from heaven's fountain sweeter
    When we awake.

## REV. SYLVANUS COBB, D.D.*

GO to thy rest, O man of God! on high,
    With those who bore the burden and the heat
Of bygone days, when Truth, that could not die,
    Burned on your lips and guided all your feet.

* Sung at the funeral in School-street Church, Boston, Mass.

We mourn thine absence from familiar ways;
  But high and pure the paths which thou hast trod:
We hope to follow till we meet and praise
  With thee and thine before the throne of God.

Long will thy name be cherished 'mid the ranks
  Of those who teach our God's undying love;
While evermore we bow with reverent thanks,
  And ask for grace to follow thee above.

Go to thy place amid the radiant host:
  We mourn thy loss from earth with tears to-day;
Yet they who knew thee best and loved thee most
  Say not, "Return," but "Speed thee on thy way!"

Rise to thy place beside the valiant few
  Who boundless grace proclaimed in days gone by:
The crown is thine; the victor's palm thy due;
  And thine the welcome where no more we die.

## EUGENE FULLER.[*]

I KNEW him not; mine eye had never gazed
  Upon his thoughtful brow:
His name, so musical, I scarce had heard
  To recognize till now.

[*] Suggested by the recent death by drowning of Eugene Fuller, Esq., brother of Margaret, Countess d'Ossoli, and of Rev. Arthur B. Fuller, and R. F. Fuller, Esq., of Boston.

But neither years nor space will now erase
    From out my heart his name;
For with his sister's it will e'er be linked,
    And share her deathless fame.

Since both have found, when homeward tending, rest
    Beneath the foamy wave,
Whereon no marble monument may stand
    To mark their watery grave.

O Sea! wert thou not satisfied to take
    The sister, good and wise,
And bear her with her loved ones to their home
    Above the starry skies?

Why shouldst thou rend again those mourning hearts,
    O dark and treacherous Sea?
Why bid those hearts forevermore be sad,
    Ocean, at sight of thee?

Hush! gentle voices to my soul are calling,
    And, whispering, they tell,
"The ocean is the Lord's; it doth his bidding;
    Repine not; all is well."

Beyond the confines of terrestrial regions,
    There is a better shore:
God's love unfathomed, as the only sea,
    Flows round it evermore.

There parted friends shall meet, and Death's dark
    wing —
    Like sea-bird's screaming shrill —
Shall never flap above the drowning forms
    Of friends beloved still.

God speed the dawning of that glorious day,
   When, sin-freed, we shall be
Where tears are wiped from every grief-dimmed
     eye,
   And where is no more sea!

---

## RICHARD F. FULLER, ESQ.

SHADES of Mount Auburn! you are dearer still,
   More reverently I tread your flowery ways,
Since he is resting there, — in whom no guile
   Was found, who needeth not my praise.
Our God hath taken him; his crown is won:
And yet 'twas hard to say, " Thy will be done!"

Nobly he toiled to aid his fellow-man;
   His brave heart to the right was ever true;
Faithful to Christ throughout his life's brief span,
   He did a life's work, though his years were few.
He bore the Temperance banner far and high;
His name among Truth's heroes will not die.

Swift was the stroke to those who mourn his loss,
   And dark indeed the cloud around his home:
In God's strength only can they bear this cross,
   Till Death, the angel, shall to them say " Come!"
Then in the land where all God's children meet,
His smile again their longing eyes shall greet.

Oh, what a rapturous greeting on that shore
    Awaited him whose treasured ones were there!
So many who had crossed the sea before,
    And in whose presence he a heaven could share.
We can but mourn our loss: to him 'twas gain
To reach that harbor from the voyage of pain.

God make us faithful, e'en as he was true;
    And, in the Christ-like pathway that he trod,
Help us to walk, till to our raptured view
    Shall rise the glory of his new abode, —
Till by the banks of Life's fair stream we stand,
And greet each other in the better land.
    1869.

## THE TREE.

[When the late Dr. William A. Alcott, well known as an author and a lecturer on hygiene, was dying at his home in Auburndale, Mass., he sent as farewell message to his only son, then in Williams College, these words, "Live for others!" — a motto he had himself nobly acted upon through life. His remains were interred in the village cemetery at West Newton, Mass.; and a large pine overshadowed his quiet resting-place, which, greatly to the regret of his friends, has been removed.]

IT stood, — a stately evergreen,
    Above an honored grave,
As if an angel-guard serene,
    From sacrilege to save.
The wild birds on its branches sang
    Each dewy, summer morn;
And cheerfully their wood-notes rang
    To welcome back the dawn.

Now hath a ruthless hand laid low
   The tree of which we tell,
Whose friendly shade no more we know
   O'er dust we loved so well.
Ah, well! — we miss the evergreen
   When snow inwraps that clay;
But 'neath a fairer tree, I ween,
   The spirit sits to-day, —

The spirit of our sainted friend,
   Whose work was nobly done;
Whose dying words, — a fitting end! —
   "For others live, my son!"
Still echo in our hearts, to make
   Our lives more true and high;
And we shall meet him when we wake
   Where none shall sin or die.

## BURIED IN THE DEEP.

NOT by his grave I stand, — loved long ago, —
   My playmate sleeping "Death's long, dreamless sleep."
He on the tossing billow met Life's foe;
   And he, alas! was buried in the deep.

No marble cenotaph, his tomb to mark,
   Can ever rise above those waves afar;
But while remains unquenched in me Life's spark,
   Still bright for me shall beam his natal star.

His birthday! it is here, and bids me turn
  To vanished hours of childhood's careless joy,
When Love's sweet lessons oft my heart could learn
  From that dear brother, that kind sailor-boy!

Now, far from that loved early home I dwell;
  No more those paths our childhood knew we tread;
Nor can we meet till I have said " Farewell
  To earthly scenes," and o'er Death's river sped.

Yet Memory, ever true, with magic wand
  Oft gilds each hour of our glad life anew;
And Faith reveals a better land beyond,
  Than e'en our island-home 'mid waters blue.

I hope to meet him on the shining shore,
  Where none of friends bereft shall lonely weep,
Where rolls no watery waste forevermore,
  Where no loved forms are buried in the deep.

## THE MOTHER OF JOHN G. WHITTIER.

SHE has passed away like the flowers of earth;
  She has faded like a star,
When the autumn winds bow the forest-leaves,
  When the day-god comes from far.

But her memory lives with loved ones left,
  Like the fragrance of a flower;
And oft in the sky of each soul shall beam,
  Like the star of the morning hour.

But not lost! oh, no! she but died to live;
  She " passed on " to die no more;
And o'er to her loved ones must she prove
  As a tie to a fairer shore.

Oh! then will the heart of her poet-son
  With his mother so loved commune;
And his sister say, with a smile of faith,
  " Let the will of the Lord be done."

O'er her spirit the soft-winged dove of peace
  In the death-hour brooded still;
And the waves of God's love, as they bathed her
    soul,
  With his joy seemed that soul to fill.

Why mourn we for those who in peace depart,
  With their heaven on earth begun?
For the trusting soul and the loving heart
  Wait the Master's words, " Well done!"

## STEPHEN GRELLET.

[Suggested by the perusal of Sebohm's interesting Memoir of this distinguished minister of the Society of Friends, lately published by Henry Longstreth, Philadelphia.]

MINE eyes ne'er looked upon his saintly brow,
  White with Life's wintry sign;
Nor have mine ears his gospel music heard,
  Sweet with the truth divine.

His birthday! it is here, and bids me turn
   To vanished hours of childhood's careless joy,
When Love's sweet lessons oft my heart could learn
   From that dear brother, that kind sailor-boy!

Now, far from that loved early home I dwell;
   No more those paths our childhood knew we tread;
Nor can we meet till I have said "Farewell
   To earthly scenes," and o'er Death's river sped.

Yet Memory, ever true, with magic wand
   Oft gilds each hour of our glad life anew;
And Faith reveals a better land beyond,
   Than e'en our island-home 'mid waters blue.

I hope to meet him on the shining shore,
   Where none of friends bereft shall lonely weep,
Where rolls no watery waste forevermore,
   Where no loved forms are buried in the deep.

## THE MOTHER OF JOHN G. WHITTIER.

SHE has passed away like the flowers of earth;
   She has faded like a star,
When the autumn winds bow the forest-leaves,
   When the day-god comes from far.

But her memory lives with loved ones left,
   Like the fragrance of a flower;
And oft in the sky of each soul shall beam,
   Like the star of the morning hour.

But not lost! oh, no! she but died to live;
    She "passed on" to die no more;
And e'er to her loved ones must she prove
    As a tie to a fairer shore.

Oh! then will the heart of her poet-son
    With his mother so loved commune;
And his sister say, with a smile of faith,
    "Let the will of the Lord be done."

O'er her spirit the soft-winged dove of peace
    In the death-hour brooded still;
And the waves of God's love, as they bathed her soul,
    With his joy seemed that soul to fill.

Why mourn we for those who in peace depart,
    With their heaven on earth begun?
For the trusting soul and the loving heart
    Wait the Master's words, "Well done!"

---

## STEPHEN GRELLET.

[Suggested by the perusal of Sebohm's interesting Memoir of this distinguished minister of the Society of Friends, lately published by Henry Longstreth, Philadelphia.]

MINE eyes ne'er looked upon his saintly brow,
    White with Life's wintry sign;
Nor have mine ears his gospel music heard,
    Sweet with the truth divine.

But yet I love him, as a blood-washed soul
    To holy service called;
And faithful ever to the inward voice,
    By none on earth appalled.

I hope to meet him on the heavenly heights,
    And hear him gently say
How he was guided by the Spirit's voice
    To Christ, the living Way.

And how, obedient to the Master's call,
    He trod the path designed,
To every pressure of a Father's hand,
    In Christian faith, resigned.

Oh wondrous faith! to traverse land and sea
    Obedient to his will
Who only to the wrathful waves can say,
    In passion's hour, " Be still."

He learned to wait upon his risen Lord,
    And in the stillness know
When to the palace, or the prisoner's cell,
    His willing feet should go.

And, as a messenger of love, he went
    And preached of Christ to those
Whose sin-worn souls the offered mercy took, —
    A solace for their woes.

In the hereafter, glorious and great
    His bright reward shall be,
To meet those souls, new-clothed, at Jesus' feet,
    From sin forever free.

Pure spirit! washed and sanctified e'en here,
  Through thee thy Master spoke;
And slumbering souls, long fellow-heirs of death,
  To God and life awoke.

I honor thee, who honored Christ my Lord,
  And wait the coming day,
When I shall tell thee how thy written words
  Oft cheered my pilgrim way.

## ONE WEEK IN HEAVEN.

[Suggested by the death of Mrs. Lydia G. Swain, of Nantucket, who "passed on" Dec. 13, 1857.]

ONE week has passed since on the earth
  Those eyes in death were closed, —
One week since she who loved our Lord
  Hath in his arms reposed.
Death could not visit such as she,
  So loving and so true,
But as a messenger, to guide
  The shadow-valley through.

Christ oped to her the golden gates
  Of everlasting day,
And pointed out to her a place
  'Mid saints in bright array.

When, only seven days ago,
   This sabbath morn, was given,
Her holiest birthday: now my friend
   Hath spent one week in heaven.

One week in heaven! Oh what bliss,
   To change the sin and pain
Which mars the earth for that bright home
   Where holiness shall reign,
Where not a pang is ever known,
   Where tears are wiped away,
Where prayer becomes eternal praise,
   And night is changed to day!

One week in heaven! Long ere this
   Dear kindred souls she's found:
While I this feeble tribute pen,
   She's treading heavenly ground
With many a wise and happy soul,
   And holds communion sweet
With those whom while on earth she hoped
   Full oft in heaven to greet.

One week in heaven! I must weep,
   To think that we no more
Shall clasp again the friendly hand
   Upon the island shore;
Yet oh! there's consolation here
   To sorrowing spirits given,
That to the saint each hour from earth
   Is so much time in heaven.

We shall not bow on earth, sweet friend,
  Before our Father's throne;
Nor meet again together where
  We've met his love to own:
But oh! there's comfort in the thought,
  That those through Jesus joined
Will meet at last, when welcomes sweet
  Are not with farewells twined.

## LITTLE JOSEY.

FAST his sands of life were passing:
  Josey knew that he must die;
And with feeble voice he whispered,
  "Would I'd been a better boy!"
Then he softly said, "Our Father,"
  Raising heavenward his eye.

"Hallowed be thy name," he whispered;
  "Kingdom come, and will be done."
Then his voice, so feeble, faltered;
  And the prayer but just begun,
He besought the dear ones round him,
  For his sake, to whisper on.

Never sought repentant sinners
  Pardon through the blessed Son,
But the voice of Jesus whispered,
  "Peace and pardon is thine own."

Weep no more for little Josey:
  His immortal crown is won.

Softly did the angels gather
  Round his love-watched couch of pain,
Soothing him till they were summoned
  To their glorious home again;
Then they bore his deathless spirit
  Up to join the heavenly train.

## "LIVE FOR OTHERS."

[The late Dr. Wm. A. Alcott, well known as a philanthropist, and the author of many works on hygiene,* when upon his death-bed sent a message to his only son, then absent at Williams College, which "reflected the animating impulse of his entire life," viz., " *To live for others.*"]

NOBLE message! truly, bravely,
  E'er the dying father strove
Thus to live and toil for others,
  With a life-long zeal and love.
Now his mantle must be yielded,
  Who should wear it but his son?
Who but he, by such a father,
  Should to such a path be won?

---

\* Dr. Alcott was the author of more than a hundred and fifty volumes, which show plainly that he lived for others.

Glorious message! when his jewels
  God shall gather from the dust,
He who such a message heedeth
  Shall be numbered with the just.
He who lives and toils for others,
  Bearing meekly every cross,
Shall be found by the Refiner
  Gold forever free from dross.

Holy message! fitly uttered
  By the dying lips of one
Who in humble self-denial
  Daily followed God's dear Son.
Let the motto, " *Live for others*,"
  On our hearts be written now;
For the unselfish spirit weareth
  Heaven's mark upon his brow.

## MAJOR SOULE.

REST, Christian soldier! for the war is o'er;
  The strife is ended with the victory gained.
Thy country needs thy loyal sword no more;
  The Union hath to Freedom's height attained.

'Tis well that she no more hath need of thee;
  For thou hast risen far beyond her call:
From sin and sorrow thou art truly free,
  Holding amid the blest high festival.

We lay our tributes at thy loyal feet;
    We crown thy head with Fame's immortal bays;
We hail thee in those bonds, so pure and sweet,
    Which bind to God through everlasting days.

Soldier and Christian! long shall Memory keep
    Thy words of patriot zeal and holy faith,
Till those who listen share thy last, long sleep,
    And rise with thee victorious over death.

God shield thy lambs, and guide them to his fold,
    Blessing their spirits, aiding them to bless,
And prove his promise, better far than gold,
    In caring for the lone and fatherless.

And when the silent boatman comes for me,
    May I, like thee, depart with holy joy, —
Launch, like thee, fearless on the unknown sea,
    And anchor where the bliss hath no alloy!

Till then I'll cherish in my loyal heart
    The memory of thy noble, stainless life,
And, while regretting thou shouldst soon depart,
    With all true patriots joy o'er ended strife.

Farewell, O Christian soldier! sweetly rest
    In the dear presence of the Prince of peace;
Waiting until thou shalt be fully blest,
    As death shall give thy loved ones their release.

## ELIOT'S MONUMENT.

'TIS well: the massive shaft should stand,
    Memorial of a by-gone day,
When apostolic Eliot preached
    To souls that long have passed away.
The spreading branches, 'neath whose shade
    The man of God so meekly stood,
Have disappeared, as Time's sharp axe
    Struck at the monarch of the wood.

But still the truths he there proclaimed,
    In all their pristine glory stay
Where once he stood; and his pure fame
    Linked to those truths shall ne'er decay.
Oh! better far the name he won
    Than those which Rome's proud conquerors wore:
Theirs was the dross which vanishes,
    And his the pure and priceless ore.

The tree has fallen which to him
    Was chapel, roof, and holy shrine;
And all that tawny forest-tribe
    Which listened, now has known decline.
The red man lingered not, but passed
    Before the white man's kingly tread;
And Natick names her Eliot
    Among her honored, speaking dead.

So may we live, that, when to us
   The scenes of earth shall be no more,
Our memories, like an echo sweet,
   Shall still remain upon this shore!
So live, that, when the Lord shall count
   Each radiant, pure, and precious gem,
We shall be numbered with the host
   That form his glorious diadem!

---

## MY FAREWELL TO 1864.

THE year is vanishing: I hear
   The sound of flying feet,
As onward haste the rapid hours
   The olden Past to greet.
What hast thou been to me, Old Year,
   So swift receding now?
Answer, O Time! for thou hast placed
   Thy wrinkles on my brow.

Thou hast taken away, O passing year!
   The loved of long ago;
Thou hast left the lips that my love hath pressed
   In the casket lying low.
And the noble youth, our household pet,
   Our brother young and brave,
Thou hast hid him, too, from our loving sight,
   Far under the distant wave.

My fair young sister! the evening breeze,
   Through the pine-trees sighing now,
Seems whispering "Mary."  O heart of mine!
   Be still, and humbly bow;
For the dear God dealt with that sister fair
   So tenderly the while,
That the tearful eyes which above her watched
   Could upward look and smile.


Old Year, thou hast garnered, too, the sheaf
   All ripe for the harvest-hour;
And the placid smile of my early guide
   I shall see on earth no more.
My father's mother! she sits not now
   In the place of silent prayer,
With her Quaker garb; but she worships still,
   And I hope to meet her there, —

There, under the roof of the temple high,
   No mortal hand hath reared,
Where the heart is free, and the worship pure,
   And no soul by sin is marred.
Oh! there I may meet her, and read again,
   As oft in the olden time,
Some word prophetic, or some high truth,
   Soft-clothed in the music rhyme.


But I pause; for hark! the winds sigh low
   And sad 'mid the pines to-night,
And I think of another dear saint who has gone
   To walk with our Lord in white.

My pastor's wife, and my heart's choice friend :
   Old Year ! I saw her die
Ere thine autumn leaves had strewn the earth ;
   But her record was on high.

God knows how sad is this heart of mine
   When I think of the loved ones gone !
God knows how sweet is the hope which cheers
   My heart as my days pass on !
Old Year, farewell ! there will dawn for me
   A bright and a glad New Year,
When my loved and lost I again shall see,
   And no more partings fear.

# POEMS OF SYMPATHY.

# POEMS OF SYMPATHY.

## A BABY BORNE AWAY.

HUSH! 'tis a little coffin, and a tiny form is there:
Only a promise-bud is plucked from out a garden fair.
Rare blossoms, full-bloomed, fragrant, and beautiful remain:
Why miss one little mignonette from out the gorgeous train?

Ah! but the babe was precious to the yearning mother's heart:
This early gathered flow'ret seemed of her own life a part;
And though the casket was so small, 'twas cast in no rough mould,
And held a jewel costlier far than El-Dorado's gold.

That baby form, so frail and weak, divinity enshrined, —
A spark of heaven's holiest fire, a young immortal mind.

Affection true and tender in its helplessness it woke ;
And tendrils round fond hearts intwined, which
    Death hath never broke.

A feeble infant once it was, a suffering, patient child ;
But now upon the shining shore, all safe and unde-
    filed,
'Twill grow a strong-winged angel, and blessings bear
    to her
Whose never-waning love will prove o'er death a
    conqueror.

That love outstretches all the little bounds of time,
And knows its only limit on that holy height sub-
    lime,
Where faith is lost in sight, and those who said
    " Farewell!"
With all they love, in bowers of bliss, forevermore
    shall dwell.

---

## TO A MOTHERLESS FRIEND.

LET me draw near thee in this hour of sadness,
    Friend of my early days!
Thou who didst send full many a ray of gladness
    Across my youthful ways.

I offer thee a cup of consolation,
    Whose taste mine heart hath known
In seasons of that spirit-desolation
    Which have been oft mine own.

Thou mournest now the absence of a mother,
    Loved, tender, wise, and true:
She hath but passed from this world to another
    Scarcely beyond thy view.

Where the dear objects that our souls have cherished
    Fade like the stars away:
Out of our sight are they, but oh! not perished,
    But lost in heaven's day.

Our eyes are weak; the mists of earth have dimmed them;
    Their chariots of fire
We see not; but with Him who hath redeemed them
    Our loved ones have gone higher.

Eyes that have looked through life with love upon us
    Have looked their last on earth:
They wait to see us when the grave that won us
    To our immortal birth.

Lift thou thy thoughts, in this dark hour, to heaven,
    And whisper, "God is love:"
He hath but taken what his love hath given
    To greater joy above.

Look up to him, and oh! may he sustain thee,
    Thou dear and stricken one!
And, by Life's discipline, through Jesus train thee,
    Till thou art all his own, —

She is in heaven! She no more may tread
   The devious paths of earth with weary feet:
Glory celestial crowns that dear one's head;
   Joy is her heritage where saved ones meet.

She is in heaven! While sadly I peruse
   Her letters filled with love to our blest Lord,
I weep, as Memory the past reviews:
   Her willing pen for me can trace no word.

She is in heaven! Oh, why should I regret
   The summons merciful which called her home!
Her cheeks no more with earth-born tears are wet:
   Oh for the hour when Christ shall bid me "Come!"

She is in heaven! Close by our Saviour's side,
   She roves amid the verdant pastures now,
Forever with her Master to abide,
   Where all with loving hearts to Jesus bow.

She is in heaven! I long to greet her there,
   Far from the snares of sin, the clouds of earth,
Her rapturous bliss at seeing God to share,
   In that safe fold of our immortal birth.

## KISS ME, MOTHER.

"KISS me, mother!" the pale lips said;
   And the glance of the loving eye
Told more than words how deep the love
   Of the maiden, called to die,

For the noble mother who bent above
    The couch of her dying child,
And smoothed the pillow with gentle words,
    And love-tones sweet and mild.


The mother bent o'er her youngest born
    With an aching heart that day;
For she knew the messenger death was near,
    To take her child away.
But she stilled the throbbing of anguish there,
    With the " hush " of a living faith, —
A faith that is strong 'mid earthly trials,
    And calm in the hour of death.


Then she kissed her child with a mother's kiss,
    How full of holy love!
And she pointed her lamb to the Lamb of God,
    And the rest of the saints above.
And the music tones of a holy hymn
    Filled the air of the quiet room
Where the Christian maiden, with faith sublime,
    Awaited her summons home.


And the Master called for his early flower
    To bloom in the garden above:
As the sabbath closed, she passed away
    To the land of sinless love.
While her young companions were met for prayer,
    Where oft she had met with them,
As they spoke of her *prayers*, she upward passed
    To *praise* with the seraphim.

Her last dear words! they will live for aye
  In that mother's faithful heart;
And many a time, by a vision stirred,
  That mother from sleep will start,
As that "Kiss me, mother!" shall echo sweet
  In memory's ears anew,
And shall bend again o'er that couch with love
  Which a mother alone can know.

O mother-heart! thou shalt throb in joy
  On the bright and shining shore;
For the "Kiss me, mother!" shall truly sound
  From that precious child once more,
As she welcomes thy coming to join the band
  Whose robes are in blood made white,
In the land where the heart is satisfied,
  On the day that knows no night.

## THE ANSWERED PRAYER.

UPON her couch of pain from day to day,
  The darling daughter and the only child
In Christian patience waited for the hour
  When Christ should call her with his voice so mild.

For she had found him precious to her soul,
  When health's bright angel from her presence fled,
And blessed the love that cheered the path of one
  So soon to be among the silent dead.

Her mother, with a Christian's holy trust,
   Resigned her daughter to her Saviour's care,
Yet listened with a mother's yearning love
   While feebly rose to heaven that daughter's prayer.

" Father in heaven ! thy will, not mine, be done ;
   Yet, if it please thee, o'er the waters dark,
For Jesus' sake, permit thy child to know
   A gentle passage for her spirit-bark."

The prayer was answered: when the summons came
   That snapped the cord which bound her soul to earth,
Soft as the zephyr was her parting breath,
   And peacefully she found immortal birth.

Now 'mid the hosts who hymn a Saviour's praise
   Her voice resoundeth, where she weeps no more ;
And those who loved her blessed the God who gave
   Such easy passage to Life's farther shore.

Not many years will pass ere they shall meet, —
   That Christian mother, and that angel child :
Then sweet will be the anthem both will sing
   For their inheritance all undefiled.

For that bright home where all God's children meet,
   Where heart greets heart in love that ne'er shall die,
And where no sin shall mar the perfect bliss
   Of those Christ welcomes to his home on high.

## TO A BEREAVED FRIEND.

WE have met like two barks upon Time's
    rushing tide:
We have parted, but oh, not forever!
Our pilot, our chart, and our haven the same:
    We shall meet, and to part again never,

In the harbor above, where the soul shall be moored,
    Far away from Life's tempest-tossed ocean;
We shall meet and rejoice where no tear dims the
    eye,
    Where the Lord whom we love is our portion.

There the dear ones who passed from our presence
    away,
    And left our hearts burdened with sorrow,
Will greet us again, and the glory enjoy
    Of that day which shall have no to-morrow.

We sigh for their presence; we long for the hour
    When our eyes shall again rest upon them;
And we almost regret that the messenger Death
    So early for heaven hath won them.

Yet deep in our heart of hearts cherish we now
    Such love to our dear risen Saviour,
That we echo his words 'mid Gethsemane's gloom,
    " Not my will, but thine, Lord, forever."

Baptized oft with suffering, and tasted the cup
    Which our Master hath drank deep before us,
With Faith's holy boldness, and Love's perfect trust,
    And the angel of prayer hovering o'er us,

We will press toward the mark; we will hope for the
    prize
Of our high and our heavenly calling;
Nor fear while we lean on the All-Father's arm,
    For he keepeth his children from falling.

---

## A MOTHER IN HEAVEN.

Though every view of heaven is fraught
    With bliss the good may share,
There's added sweetness in the thought,
    "We have a mother there."

We feel her life-long truth and love,
    Her reverence for the right,
Prepared her for a home above,
    And leaves her memory bright.

As summer breezes softly float
    O'er mead and flowery dell,
So to our hearts her earnest words,
    Remembered, oh, so well!

They linger in our memory now,
    As tones of music sweet,
And will as gems be cherished e'er,
    Till we again shall meet.

Whate'er her task in early life
    To curb each wayward will,
We prospered in the noble strife,
    And mother loves us still.

How blest the thought that mother dear,
    On yonder heavenly shore,
Each sweet, familiar voice shall hear
    Of loved ones gone before!

God of the orphan! now to thee
    Shall praise from each be given,
To whom may come the soothing thought,
    "My mother is in heaven."

## ONLY AND WELL-BELOVED.

AN only child, the household pet and joy,
    The idol of her home,
How can we say, 'twas well that she should die,
    A bud forbade to bloom!

How, but with faith that He who sees the end,
    From every opening hour,
Hath with the kindness of a loving Friend,
    With wisdom as with power,

This sweet one gathered to the angel-band,
    To sing forever there,
In the rich music of the better land,
    Peaceful and blest as fair!

God gave his Only and his Well-beloved,
    To die upon the cross:
Oh, let our spirits, every fear removed,
    Count gain what earth calls loss!

Earth with its sorrows is no more to her,
    Who sinless heights hath gained:
The bliss secured by Christ the Conqueror
    She early hath attained.

And safe upon the glad and peaceful shore,
    The well-beloved may rest:
God loves and guards our dear one evermore,
    And yet will make us blest,

When we have followed him by faith a while,
    With a re-union hour,
Where sin can nevermore our hearts beguile,
    And death has lost his power.

# MISCELLANEOUS POEMS.

# MISCELLANEOUS POEMS.

## "NO TURNING BACK."

[The Rev. Dr. Hamlin, in his interesting discourse on Religious Liberty in Turkey, delivered at the South Church, Salem, on the afternoon of Sunday, March 17, 1861, gave the following as the purport of a note secretly sent from one small band of persecuted Christians in Turkey to another company in similar circumstances: "We are seven men, faithful and true. There is death, but no turning back." This concise but comprehensive missive has suggested the following lines:]

WHY should we turn? the desert is behind us;
    Before us only lies the goodly land,
Where verdant fields and shady rills will 'mind us,
    By blissful contrast, of burning sand.

Why should we turn? the joys of earth are fleeting;
    Each gorgeous bubble bursts before our eyes:
Unfading joys in heaven are awaiting
    Those who press onward to obtain the prize.

Why should we turn? friends dearly loved and cher-
    ished
Have passed before us to the world of light:
Ne'er from our hearts has their sweet memory per-
    ished;
We wait to meet them on the heavenly height.

Why should we turn? e'en though the way is weary,
　　And steep and rugged, yet we'll struggle on:
Christ wore the thorns, his earthly path was dreary;
　　We follow thee, thou lowly, suffering one.

Why should we turn? death may be just before us;
　　Yet there's no turning back for Christ's dear flock.
What though the gathering tempest should burst o'er us,
　　We shall be sheltered 'neath Salvation's rock.

*We will not turn!* We welcome Death's dark billow:
　　'Twill bear us on to our loved Master's side;
We share his calmness who his head could pillow
　　Amid the storms o'er the Galilean tide.

*We will not turn!* On, on, we hasten gladly,
　　Counting the hours before our change shall come:
How can we journey onward slowly, sadly,
　　When just before us is our heavenly home!

---

## THE MUSIC OF THE PINES.

ON a day in the early autumn time,
　　I roamed with a friend afar,
Where the ebon berries, and the orchis fair,
　　And the lofty pine-trees are.

Oh, the music roar of the forest-pine,
   How it filled my heart with glee,
As it brought to mem'ry's view the hours
   Of my childhood by the sea!

The feathery fern by the mossy rock
   In its wild luxuriance grew;
And the trailing vines of the blackberry swept
   In the tangled pathway new;
And the music-voice of the forest-pines
   Filled the air with melody,
Like the roar of the cataract's waters grand,
   Or the sound of the distant sea.

There the fragrant *saxifraga* rose
   By the whortleberry's side,
In the welcome shade of the lofty trees,
   Where the zephyrs cool abide;
And the verdurous plumes of the forest pines
   Swift waved in their murmurous glee;
And my heart went back to my childhood's home
   And the voice of its sounding sea.

There the song of the forest-bird was heard
   From the bough far-off and high,
And the whistle clear of the farmer's boy
   As he came our pathway nigh;
But the solemn voice of the murmurous pines
   Was the sweetest sound to me,
As it brought to mind those earlier hours
   By its roar like the distant sea.

When the ransomed gather in bliss at last,
   Where the sea shall roll no more,
Say, how shall the heart be satisfied
   That was born on an island shore?
Oh, the music-roar of the forest-pines
   May be heard from Life's fair tree,
And its healing leaves have a murmurous voice,
   Like the sound of the distant sea!

## THE RECEDING COMET.

THOU radiant traveller through the realms of space,
   We welcomed thee, as to our startled eyes
Thy shining nucleus and thy silvery train
   Gave their effulgence to our evening skies.

Thou hast made yet more beautiful to us
   Night's glittering canopy; and filled our souls
With wonder at His power whose fiat high
   Woke thee to being, and thy course controls.

Now thou'rt receding from our feeble sight,
   Of other worlds to glance athwart the skies:
Go! and awake to wonder other souls,
   Till praise to God from them shall also rise.

God the Creator! Wonder-working Power!
   Seen in the glorious works his hand hath made;
God the Upholder! in the robes of might
   And wisdom infinite for aye arrayed.

Our spirits praise him as the King of kings,
   Incomprehensible as he is good.
Thou flaming visitant, we know thee not:
   How by our searchings can we find out God?

Yet go, bright voyager, to other worlds,
   And tell the praises which from sea to sea,
To him who spread thy banner on the sky,
   Have risen from human hearts at sight of thee.

## MY MOTHER'S VOICE IN PRAYER.

I'VE heard her oft at the midnight hour,
   When all was still beside,
And her voice alone on the silent air
   Like music seemed to glide;
And I've hushed my breath to listen then,
   In the holy silence there:
Oh! I never, never, can forget
   My mother's voice in prayer.

I've heard her oft in my early days,
   As she knelt beside my bed;
And I almost feel, this very hour,
   Her hand upon my head.
I remember how I wondered then,
   If angels hovered near;
And in my inmost soul I loved
   My mother's voice in prayer.

I've seen her bowed in the holy place
    Where the saints were met to pray,
And close with the echoing song of praise
    The holy sabbath day.
I know by the gleaming of many an eye
    Her form was welcome there,
And many a heart with mine has hailed
    My mother's voice in prayer.

She has knelt by the bed of the dying saint,
    As he drew near the shadowy vale,
And spoke of the promises dear and true,
    Lest his faith in the Lamb should fail;
And the Master listened, I know, to her
    Who knelt 'mid the sobbings there,
While the parting soul in triumph heard
    My mother's voice in prayer.

I've heard her pray, in this trial hour,
    For the land she loves the best,
That the dove of Peace might fold its wings
    Once more on Freedom's breast.
She asked that the sons of worthy sires
    For her might the armor wear, —
Ah! my country's call is blending with
    My mother's voice in prayer.

I go to the field with a hopeful heart;
    My mother has kissed me "Good-by:"
She will greet me with joy if I'm spared to return,
    And smile through her tears if I die.

And I shall remember her in the camp,
   And follow her teachings there;
For no siren song can drown the tones
   Of my mother's voice in prayer.

When the scenes of battle mine eye shall view,
   And the shot and shell fly fast,
I shall think of mother, her parting words,
   And her look when I saw her last.
And afar above all the noise of strife,
   Lifting off from my soul its care,
I shall hear, as the angels hear on high,
   My mother's voice in prayer.

To my latest hour will those precious tones
   In my memory sweetly sound,
While I walk the earth, and when, saved by Christ,
   With the ransomed I am found.
Oh, yes! while the music of raptured saints
   Stirs ever the heavenly air,
I shall hear in the chambers of my soul
   My mother's voice in prayer.

---

## TO A DAFFODIL.

GOD did not give to thee the beauty of the rose,
   Nor yet the fragrance of the violet sweet,
Yet named thee as a flower which early blows,
   Among the first returning spring to greet.

Then hail to thee, thou golden daffodil!
   Though of delusive hope thou art the sign,
Truth is the same, whoe'er the pulpit fill:
   Love's token only is this flower of mine.

Thou art the earliest blossom which to me
   From friendly hands hath borne a message sweet,
Since spring hath called the bird and flower and bee
   To gladden earth with song and beauty meet.

Welcome, thrice welcome, as the gift of one
   Who would send sunshine into every heart,
And bid the tearful think of that glad morn
   When God himself shall say to grief, "Depart."

Around her earthly path may flowers of love,
   Of peace and hope, in fadeless colors bloom!
And may she gather, where the angels rove,
   Those amaranths that grow beyond the tomb!

## THE STUDENT'S PRAYER.

*"In every thing by prayer and supplication, with thanksgiving, let your requests be made known unto God."—*PHIL. iv. 6.

O THOU who gavest me those mental powers
   By which thy words and works I may peruse,
Be ever near me in those study-hours,
   Which, with delight, from other toil I choose.
The volume once by inspiration given,
The chart by which to cross Life's sea to heaven;

And that glad book of Nature, spread abroad,
Which tells in voiceless eloquence of God, —
Oh help me faithfully to study these,
As one who on each page thy goodness sees!

When, with a reverent spirit, I shall take
   The book divine to con its lessons o'er,
Dear Master, bid my soul to joy awake,
   As thy rich love shall be my garnered lore;
And let the record of thy spotless life
Inspire me for the earnest Christian strife,
And every wise requirement of my Lord
Be written on my heart as in thy word,
While Memory shall thy promises retain,
To calm my fears, and soothe each mental pain.

When o'er the classic page in ancient tongue,
   I muse on heroes of the twilight-time,
May all the melody of Homer's song,
   And Virgil's music, in their pleasant rhyme,
My memory quicken when my pen essays
To write an anthem, Father, to thy praise,
And each high attribute to their gods given
I then may claim for thee, O King of heaven!
And every virtue heroes there displayed
Declare but dust when 'gainst my Saviour's weighed.

When in the languages still used by men,
   In lands beyond the waters wide and lone,
I strive to speak, and grasp within my ken
   The lore of other countries than my own,
Oh give me wisdom to discern the true,
Nor let me gather thorns, but blossoms strew

Around my mental path, that I may twine
Some chaplet from those countries worthy mine, —
Gain knowledge from their stores which shall impart
New vigor to my mind, wake new love in my heart!

When pondering over problems in my task,
　While Euclid I essay to demonstrate,
While algebraic signs, like puzzles, ask
　That I the true equation e'er should make,
Then quicken thou my mind for vigorous thought,
Assist me to untie each Gordian knot,
And let the mathematics, e'en the abstract,
Assist to make my moral self exact;
Then shall I safely tread Life's labyrinth way,
Following the clew which leads to endless day.

When on the page of history I read
　The deeds of men upon thy footstool, Lord!
Each bright example may my spirit heed,
　And be the sins of heroes e'en, abhorred.
As sacred History shall Thee proclaim,
Great Leader of the hosts that owned thy name!
May I respond to every word of praise,
And seek thee as the Guide of all my ways,
While every record of each tribe and land
Awakes the thought of thy controlling hand!

All, all, my hours of study consecrate,
　Great Source of wisdom! and each lesson bless
To my aspiring spirit, till they make
　My mind as well as heart thy law confess.
Then, like a hero in his armor clad,

Bid me, in learning's panoply arrayed,
Go forth to wage successfully the war
Which wisdom doth with ignorance declare,
While, with the knowledge which makes truly wise,
I point immortal spirits to the skies.

## TO MARIA MITCHELL.

THE bright waves glancing, beckon thee away,
    And other lands are calling thee from home:
Receive in kindness now this simple lay,
    Ere thou in far and foreign climes shall roam.

I bid thee go: my heart exults with thee,
    That soon thy feet may press a distant shore:
Our mother-country, England, thou shalt see,
    And view her smiling fields and ruins hoar.

On Alpine heights ere long perchance thou'lt stand,
    And view with pleasure beauty's landscape wide;
May tread the storied haunts of classic land,
    And float upon the Rhine's or Arno's tide.

But, wheresoe'er thou goest, may the Power
    Which bids the orbs of heaven in order move
Protect and guide and bless thee every hour,
    Till thou shalt cease afar from home to rove!

May Peace her white wings fold upon thy heart,
    As o'er the billowy deep thy bark shall glide;
And all with whom thou, sorrowing, must part,
    Be spared to greet thee on the homeward side!

In rich communion with the wise afar,
   Mayst thou full many a happy season spend,
While the fair lustre of thy natal star
   Shall with their radiance ever calmly blend!

Farewell! our paths on earth may seldom meet;
   Our orbits ne'er again may cross below;
But I shall e'er thy name with pleasure greet,
   And ask that laurel-wreaths thy path may strew.

But, better far, Maria, may thy name
   Be written fair upon the heavenly scroll,
That thus thou mayst possess eternal fame,
   And reach at last ambition's highest goal!

There may we meet; there may I tell to thee
   What these few lines but feebly may impart,
That, while my youth shall dwell in memory,
   I will remember thee with grateful heart!

Farewell, once more! health's angel thee attend,
   And with its wings full often fan thy brow;
And every soul that greets thee prove a friend,
   Till thou shalt meet the friends thou leavest now.

---

## BRANT POINT.

HAUNT of my childhood, I can ne'er forget
      Those pleasant hours of yore,
When free from care, and with a bounding step,
      I trod that sandy shore.

There have I gambolled oft in childhood's glee,
    Climbing each sandy hill,
Gathering fair shells and wave-worn pebbles bright,
    Watching each snowy sail.

I ever loved in Nature's book to trace
    The proof of love divine,
And oft, as on illuminated page,
    See truest wisdom shine.

And there I saw, in pebble and in shell,
    In wave and fish and weed,
Those tokens of God's presence, which I crave
    To meet my spirit's need.

Nor only on the sandy shore I found
    Enjoyment pure and sweet,
But gladly up the far-seen beacon tower
    Went oft my youthful feet.

And there, with trap-door closed, I read,
    From human ears afar,
The wondrous words of Avon's bard, and those
    Which traced Childe Harold's star.

Round the great lantern swept the ocean blast,
    My childish voice to drown;
Far off before me stretched the mighty deep;
    Behind, my native town.

Gone is that lighthouse now, its inmates gone:
    A fairer structure stands,
To guide the mariner in safety o'er
    Those shifting, dangerous sands.

And scattered are the friends who with me there
    Knew many a happy day;
Some, from that isle to heaven's serener shore,
    Forever passed away.

But in my heart the memories remain
    Of that sweet, olden time;
So, grateful, I, within a far-off home,
    Embalm Brant Point in rhyme:

Content, if some who oft have wandered there
    With me in days agone
Shall read these lines with loving thought of one
    Who, absent, yet loves on;

And, though Nantucket's star may seem to set,
    Thanks God for what *has been*
In days of yore, whose visions linger yet,
    Robed in affection's sheen.

---

## DEAD HOPES.

THE dead leaves strew my daily paths,
    And dead hopes strew my heart.
Alas! that autumn storms must come,
    And summer joys depart;
Alas! that prospects bright as morn
Should fade like day when eve comes on.

The cherished hope of early years,
   Too bright for earth to hold,
The gay, glad promise of my youth,
   The flower that would unfold,
Now, withered like the autumn leaves,
No more my trusting heart deceives.

I walk henceforth beneath the cloud;
   My heart is shrouded now:
Yet, meekly, Father, to thy will,
   That aching heart would bow.
Sunshine, thank God! is on my head,
Since only earthly hopes are dead.

What though the forms I loved so well
   Are sleeping 'neath the sod!
What though the spirits once with me
   Are walking now with God,
In that bright land where angels sing,
And bloom the flowers of endless spring!

There comes a day my soul shall know,
   When all I hoped for here,
Forever fresh, forever bright,
   Shall be my portion there:
All that the Father gives the Son
Shall share the joys by angels known.

The dead leaves in my daily path
   Will one day disappear;
And vernal beauty clothe the earth,
   And summer joys draw near:
So will my heart, of earth's hopes riven,
Bloom with the unfading hopes of heaven.

## ANGELIC LANGUAGE.

> "The angels, in like manner, can utter in a few words singular the things which are written in a volume of any book, and can express such things, or every word, as elevate its meaning to interior wisdom; for their speech is such, that it is consonant with affections, and every word with ideas. Expressions are also varied, by an infinity of methods, according to the series of the things which are in a complex in the thought." — SWEDENBORG.

HOW faint and feeble are the words we speak
When deep emotions in our souls awake!
How vainly do we strive our inmost heart
To friends on earth by language to impart!
When, heavenly *Logos!* will the hour draw nigh
That angel-language will our need supply?

Oft have my lips to silence been compelled,
Because the love, which from deep fountains welled
For cherished friends, had utterance denied;
Since earth hath not that language, deep and wide,
Yet comprehensive, which those bright ones know
Who dwell in bliss where soon we hope to go.

Oft as my soul has bowed in solemn prayer,
I've sought to speak its adoration there,
And sighed in vain for that live, burning coal
Which touched the poet-prophet's lips of old,
And yet rejoiced that Christ could read my heart,
And knew the worship language failed t'impart.

There comes a day, my spirit joys to know,
When thought and utterance side by side shall flow:

Both from the fount of the affections spring,
And each the wealth of heavenly wisdom bring.
O blessed Master! bring me to that land
Where those I love my heart shall understand.

Guide me, oh, guide me! o'er Life's waters dark,
Till moored in heaven is my spirit bark,
Where, with angelic language, I may tell
My love for him who "doeth all things well,"
Life's stormy gales to heavenly zephyrs lulled,
And all my soul by perfect love controlled.

## ON THE SHORE OF THE SOUNDING SEA.

AIR. — "*Banks of the Blue Moselle.*"

OH! I'd love to wander a while, my friend,
    Far away and alone with thee,
"In the starry light of a summer night,"
    On the shore of the sounding sea.
And I'd joy to hear from thy lips, my friend,
    Words of love that are dear to me,
While thy soulful tones blend with ocean's moans,
    On the shore of the sounding sea.

Oh! I'd love to look in thine eyes, my friend,
    And there read of thy love for me;
And a sister's smile should my heart beguile,
    On the shore of the sounding sea.

And we'd talk, as we noticed the gleam afar,
   Where the beacon-light burns free,
Of the faith we share, as we wander there,
   On the shore of the sounding sea.

And we'll kneel on the sands while the stars shine bright;
   And we'll pray that we each may be
As a beacon-light in some traveller's night,
   On the shore of Life's sounding sea;
And we'll talk of the land where the angels dwell,
   Of the home where we long to be, —
Where loved ones greet, and the parted meet,
   On the shore of Eternity's sea.

Ere we leave the spot we will breathe a prayer, —
   I for thee, and thou, love, for me, —
That our love may endure when we meet no more
   On the shore of the sounding sea;
And as home we turn from the pebbly beach,
   Where we oft have joyed to be,
Our hearts will be light, and our hopes be bright,
   On the shore of the sounding sea.

## VIOLETS.

IN that parterre toward which our steps are tending,
   The violets never die:
Let us with joy our pilgrim way be wending,
   To greet their bloom on high.

Sweet friend! my heart's best thanks to thee are given
    For every violet blue:
Sweet early blooms! how oft they speak of heaven,
    And all things fair and true!

They tell of One whose promise is unfailing:
    Spring-time hath surely come;
So, Life's long winter o'er, we shall be hailing,
    As promised, heaven's glad bloom.

Type of the spirit from the rough world shrinking,
    Hiding in lowly bed,
The dews of heaven with a glad heart drinking,
    Though bowed the reverent head.

How — more than a royal giver! — is it spending
    Its fragrance on the air,
Asking no homage, but its good-will sending
    Like sunshine everywhere.

Thank God for violets with their blue-eyed beauty,
    Fair heralds of the spring!
Would that, like theirs, it might be our high duty
    Glad tidings thus to bring!

## THE AUTUMN RAIN.

LIST! the autumn rain is falling,
    Pattering on the withered leaves,
On the brilliant autumn blossoms,
    On the farmer's golden sheaves.

Summer's glorious reign is over;
    Now the storm-clouds come again:
Cold and sad, forlorn and dreary,
    Sounds once more the autumn rain.

On the new-made graves 'tis falling, —
    Heavy drops, so chill and sad!
Changed indeed from showers of spring-time,
    Heralding the blossoms glad.
Dreary days of leaf-strewn pathways!
    Quickly have you come again:
Aching hearts can never welcome,
    Chill and drear, the autumn rain.

Close the door, and lift the curtains;
    Light anew the parlor fire:
Round those graves our spirits linger,
    And we scarce can lift them higher.
Ope the Book, the best, the dearest;
    Read each precious promise o'er;
Think! no autumn rain is falling
    On the bright and cloudless shore.

There the dear ones wait our coming;
    There the blossoms fadeless blow;
There the streams of joy celestial
    From unfailing fountains flow;
There anew the links are woven
    Of Love's bright eternal chain;
There the griefs of earth are over,
    With the dreary autumn rain.

## CHARLOTTE BRONTÉ READING THE BIBLE.

"Last Sunday, I took up my Bible in a gloomy state of mind. I began to read. A feeling stole over me such as I have not known for long years, — a sweet, placid sensation, like those I remember which used to visit me when I was a little child, and, on Sunday evenings in summer, stood by the open window, reading the life of a certain French nobleman, who attained a purer and higher degree of sanctity than has been known since the days of the early martyrs." — *Memoirs of Charlotte Bronté.*

'TWAS holy time: the winter sun gleamed coldly from the skies,
And in the heart few summer thoughts could easily arise.
The birds were wanting from the groves the list'ning ear to charm;
The chilly atmosphere almost forbade the heart to warm.
And, in this cold and dreary time, a maiden 'gan to read,
Her heart depressed, her soul benumbed, and none her state to heed.
But, from on high, a Father saw; his book was in her hand,
And swiftly o'er her soul he sent airs from the better land:
They wafted peace and joy to her the motherless and lone,
And cheered her with an influence which she had seldom known.

Long years had passed since she had breathed that aroma sublime:
It brought back vanished memories of hours in summer time,
When, as a child, she read a book by casement opened wide;
And sweet, bright visions cheered her soul at sabbath eventide.
What book was that whose pages had a charm for childhood's hour?
'Twas e'en a record of a life so holy, that its power
Was felt in plastic childhood's time as if a magi's rod,
And proved the channel through which came the glorious peace of God:
So now, as reading in the book, which, more than all beside,
Tells how the holy-hearted have for others lived and died,
Those fragrant zephyrs, from the land where flowerets never fade,
Around her spirit, as of yore, in welcome sweetness played.
Nor can we wonder; for the book was redolent of heaven,
With its story of the Crucified, through whom are sins forgiven;
With its record of the wondrous works our God on earth hath wrought,
And its revelations of the land with radiant glory fraught.
Oh! when our hearts, with gloom o'ercast, shrink from the winter sky,

And oft we wish Hope's summer day could evermore
    be nigh,
How like dear, soothing angels come those promises
    sublime
Which speak of happier days for us, beyond the
    bounds of Time!
Well might the gifted lady oft its holy pages read,
And gather strength and hope and joy for her deep
    spirit-need:
For to the soul which seeketh light from its rich, varied lore
Shall calm and holy peace and joy be given evermore;
And whether read in winter's cold, or 'mid the summer's heat,
Will bear to all who read in faith an influence pure
    and sweet.

## DEATH IN THE STATE HOUSE.*

> "Leaves have their time to fall,
> And flowers to wither in the north wind's breath,
>   And stars to set; but all,
> Thou hast all seasons for thine own, O Death!"
>                   MRS. HEMANS.

AS Indian archer in the Western wilds
    Oft sends an arrow to the timid deer,
Who, unsuspecting, at the rippling stream
    Quaffs the cold water with no thought of fear,—

---

* Suggested by the recent death of Hon. James Clark of Boston, who was listening to a debate in the Hall of Representatives, at the Massachusetts State House, at the time of his decease.

So Death, with well-filled quiver at his back,
    And bow well strung, his barbed missive sends
When least the victim dreams of danger near,
    And sips the nectar of swift hours with friends.

At home, abroad, on sea, on land, the cry,
    "Come to the Spirit Land!" alike is heard;
Nor youth, nor age, may lightly heed the call,
    Howe'er that voice the spirit may have stirred.

Within the halls of legislative fame,
    One noble patriot met the conqueror, Death;
That "old man eloquent,"* whose utterance true
    Expressed content with his expiring breath.

And now within the stately, massive walls
    Of that fair structure, Massachusetts' pride!
Beneath that dome, the Tri-mount City's crown,
    With sudden summons hath a good man died.

But shall these halls to us be filled with gloom,
    Since through them Death may glide, unheard, unseen,
And proveth thus all places, scenes, and times
    Are his for reaping, his for triumphing?

Oh, no! the place is hallowed where he treads
    Who breaks the bonds which bind a soul to earth.
That terrene spot henceforth is glorified
    From whence a spirit had its heavenly birth.

---

\* Hon. John Quincy Adams died in the Capitol at Washington. His last words were, "This is the last of earth: I am content."

Death in the State House! If an archer he,
  Who strikes the unsuspecting with his dart,
Not less a liberator is the power
  Which opes the pearly gates to each true heart.

Death in the State House! Let the brave hearts left
  To fight the battles still of human life
Be warned by this event to gird anew
  Their spirit-armor for the moral strife.

So whether called from earth 'mid home's sweet rest,
  Or 'mid the whirl of business or its care,
His coming shall be welcome, who shall lift
  The veil which hides the bliss we long to share.

## THE CHILD'S MESSAGE.

[It is stated by some writer, that a little girl was present at the funeral of a young companion. She had never looked upon a lifeless body. The coffin was surrounded with flowers tastefully arrayed, and the sleeping infant within looked lovely as if in slumber. The little girl, who was lifted up to look at it, suddenly leaned over, kissed the cheek of the sleeper, whispering in childish accents, "Give my love to God." This little incident is but paraphrased in the following lines:—]

BY parental kindness sheltered,
  Ne'er the little child had seen
One whose form of lifeless beauty
  Wore Death's sad and solemn mien;
Till a youthful, loved companion
  Soared to seek an angel's home,
And the little girl was lifted
  To behold her lifeless form.

Then the child, no death-scene fearing,
    Gazed upon the flowers around,
Wondering that from lips so lovely
    Came no pleasant, wonted sound;
Bent she o'er the tiny coffin, —
    Sunshine all her face abroad, —
Kissed the cheek of marble coldness,
    Whispering, " Give my love to God! "

Thus, if childlike each in spirit,
    We in childlike trust may bend
O'er the couch where Death is calling
    Some beloved and cherished friend;
And, while Faith's unclouded vision
    Sees them soar to heavenly rest,
Send, as if to far-off country,
    Loving message to the blest.

## THE CHILDREN'S CONCERT.

I SAW them in their snowy robes, with wreaths of evergreen
Around each youthful brow intwined, a rare and lovely scene;
While o'er their heads the flaming arch reminded of the throne,
With glorious rainbow round about, where Jesus sits alone.

Around, above, festooned or free, our country's flag appeared,
And brilliant flowers and garlands green the vision sweetly cheered.
I saw it all, a fairy scene! I heard the organ's swell;
And silvery voices sounded forth, clear as a chiming bell.
I heard the song of praise to Him who sits enthroned on high,
And thought the children looked as if but just from yonder sky.
"The Dear Old Flag" I heard them sing, and saw their banners wave,
While suddenly our ensign dropped above the fair and brave;
And while from many an eye the tear unbidden started there,
Quick from my spirit bounded forth the utterance of prayer.

"O God! preserve our country in this her trial-time,
And bid the bell of Liberty ring out its loudest chime,
Till North and South and East and West in righteousness agree,
And morning's sun and evening's stars shine only on the free.
Then will our flag, now truly loved, be dearer than before,
And, in its beauty, wave above a glad and peaceful shore."

The evening sped, the music ceased, the children
    passed away;
But in full many a listener's heart the echoes sweet
    will stay,
And many a fervent prayer ascend, that to each child
    be given
A place amid the angel-choirs that sing the songs of
    heaven.

## FLOWERS.

BRIGHT emanations of creative will,
  How oft with pleasure ye my bosom fill!
How oft to thoughts sublime ye call my soul,
While wayward fancy bends to your control!

Ye speak of friends, the distant and the dear,
And bid sweet memories my spirit cheer;
Ye call to mind the souls that soared away
To God's own garden in Life's early day.

As fragrant as your perfume now to me
Come memories o'er Life's rapid, changeful sea,
When, with the lovers of your beauty rare,
In youth's gay scenes my soul had joyous share.

Ye glorious teachers of high truths divine,
Who speak of love, and bid no soul repine,
As to the stars, to you, "earth's stars," is given
A power to win the human soul to heaven.

While praises for God's gifts to man ascend,
May praise with your uprising incense blend,
And man rejoice that flowers his path may strew,
Till ended is the race begun below.

While heavenly breezes fan the ransomed brow,
While souls redeemed before their Saviour bow,
Amid archangel songs and seraph lays,
For flowers on earth may mortals offer praise!

## NIAGARA.

AWE-STRUCK I stand
Beside this avalanche of waves, and hear
The voice of God from out these watery depths.
Emotion-full, my soul in vain essays
To speak the thoughts that by this scene have birth.
Hark! to the voice of many waters here:
Like that great voice in Patmos heard by John,
It speaks of power, resistless energy,
And mighty purpose unconfined by man.
To me it speaks of God's almighty love,
Forever surging round the human soul:
The rocks of sin, the shoals of ignorance,
But bid those waves of love in tumult rise,
In rapids like old ocean's storm-waves, or, as here,
In one vast water-sheet, the cataract's plunge.
Thus shall it flow till time shall be no more,
And every soul is borne upon its waves,
All cleansed by its pure waters, to the land
Where, joyful, they shall all be moored at last.

## GOSPEL CONSOLATION.

*" Only with silence as a benediction
God's angels come,
When in the shadow of a great affliction
The soul sits dumb."*
— WHITTIER.

How hard to walk in sorrow's echoing chambers,
    E'en with uncovered feet!
How hard to speak amid severe affliction
    E'en words of comfort sweet!

What can we say when bitter tears are falling
    From a fond mother's eyes,
Since one whose baby-form lay in her bosom
    Now in the deep sea lies?

No words can give that wrung heart consolation
    Save His of old who spake
To the sad sister of his friend departed, —
    "Thy brother shall awake."

This thought, then, only, to thee do I offer, —
    A balm for thy torn heart, —
Our loved ones die not, when, the body sleeping,
    Their souls to new life start.

They live whom now we mourn, — aye, live more truly
    Than we who here may sing,
Far from our Father's house, the songs of Zion,
    With drooping, folded wing.

There comes a day, — my spirit hails its dawning, —
    When, fetterless and free,
Our souls shall grasp the idea of the mansion
    Where all God's children be.

In God's great hand each child of earth is lying:
    He loveth every soul.
Christ died for all; and, o'er the heights of glory,
    Eternal anthems roll

From souls redeemed by him who hears to answer
    Each fervent, faith-breathed prayer;
And we may hope to meet, through grace and mercy,
    All, all, our loved ones there.

## THOUGHTS AFTER A SNOW-STORM.

I DO not love the snow: it softly falls
Like an angelic footstep on our paths,
    But it divideth me
From those I love; and, though its starry flakes
Of geometric beauty charm my eye,
    I wish it soon away.

Sweet are the airs of spring: the warm, bright days,
So welcome to the winter-wearied hearts,
    Are ever hailed by me,
The herald of the long, bright summer hours,
With floral loveliness and song of birds,
    And leafy shrub and tree.

And oh, how welcome to this heart of mine
The lingering glory of the autumn days!
  When earth seems newly clad
In robes of royalty; and on our paths
The golden-rod and aster speak of heaven,
  And all things pure and glad.

And these bright hours, how do they cheer the heart
Amid Life's many cares and burdens great!
  How speak they oft to me
Of other years, in God's great future held,
Sweet foretaste of some better days to come,
  The Eden yet to be!

But thou, O Father of the human soul!
The green earth lies beneath thy plastic hand,
  And the pure, feathery snow,
Falling all softly through the wintry day,
Obeys thy high behests, as do the flowers
  That on earth's carpet glow.

Man must breast storm, or be a pygmy still;
And only puny souls that would not grow
  Will sigh when called to bear
Or buffet: they who would be grand
And noble pillars in thy temple fair
  Must joy and sorrow share, —

Must bear the cross the glorious crown to win;
Must tread the thorny path to gather blossoms sweet
  At last in Eden's bowers;
And looking upward through the blinding snow,
Or leaping o'er its barricades in faith,
  Wait for the golden hours.

So do I wait: O soul of mine, be still!
Life hath its promise of fruition sweet,
    When, in God's clearer sight,
The fulness of our time shall fully come,
And Love shall conquer, and the tyrant wrong
    Shall be subdued by right.

## EAGLE ROCK AND MANCHESTER BEACH.

[Suggested by a picture of the sea-shore at Manchester, Mass., by George Southward.]

LIKE a strong soul it stands, while, wildly foaming,
    The billows dash around,
Till on the sandy beach they break majestic,
    With loud and solemn sound.

Well for Columbia's bird may others name it,
    Whose eyrie is on high:
For me it is the emblem of a spirit
    Strengthened to do or die.

And, as I gaze upon the glowing canvas,
    Mine heart exults to know
Such types of Nature's grand and solemn lessons
    The artist oft may show.

For he who paints the sunset's glowing amber
    Or gorgeous crimson hue,
To lift the heart towards the Celestial City,
    Its radiance to show, —

He preaches well as he who from the pulpit
    Proclaims salvation free.
God's altars need such ministers; for Nature
    Speaketh, O Christ! of thee.

Now, by sweet contrast, scenes like this before me
    Tell of that home so blest,
When hushed to peace, as waves of Galilee,
    No wave shall rear its crest.

And that strong soul, that, like a rock unshaken,
    Upon the storms looked down,
Calm amid raging billows of affliction,
    Shall wear a conqueror's crown.

God whom I serve! I thank thee for the lesson
    The artist here hath given:
Help me to heed it amid earth's commotions,
    Till I find rest in heaven.

## ELI BEN ISRAEL.

ELI BEN ISRAEL, weary with his toil,
    And heavy-hearted from continual grief,
One evening bowed beneath a stately palm,
    And, weeping, prayed to Yahveh for relief.

His words were simple, but his prayers sincere,
    And offered in the faith that wavers ne'er;
So, like an angel, from the earth it sped,
    Nor paused its pinion till it reached God's ear.

The tropic sun went swiftly down the west;
   And, as the shadows hastened o'er the plain,
Sweet was the slumber weary Eli found,
   While o'er him hung\* night's queen with starry train.

Then came a vision to the sleeper's gaze,
   A dream of comfort to his burdened soul:
He saw the end of all his toil on earth,
   And read his name on Life's illumined scroll.

A fairer city than Jerusalem
   Before his eyes in Orient splendor stood;
And angels, clad like rays of morning light,
   Smiled on him as they sang the praise of God.

A voice whose clarion tones were sweet and glad
   Then spake to him, "Oh, wait in patience still!
The soul that would enjoy supernal bliss
   Must bravely do, and calmly bear God's will.

Thy toil on earth will fit thee for thy rest,
   Thy suffering purge thy heart from all its dross:
Lo! angels walk unseen with every soul
   Which seeks eternal gain through earthly loss."

---

\* "An Oriental sky has a peculiarity which adds very much to its impressive appearance. With us, the stars seem to adhere to the face of the heavens: they form the most distant objects within the range of vision; they appear to be set in a groundwork of thick darkness, beyond which the eye does not penetrate. Unlike this is the canopy which night spreads over the traveller in Eastern climes. The stars there seem to hang like burning lamps, midway between heaven and earth; the pure atmosphere enables us to see a deep expanse of blue ether lying far beyond them. The hemisphere above us glows and sparkles with innumerable fires, that appear as if kept burning in their position by an immediate act of the Omnipotent, instead of resting on a frame-work which subserves the illusion of seeming to give them their support." — *Prof. Hackett's Illustrations of Scripture.*

He woke! — glad Eli! — with his soul refreshed,
   And trod his weary way with hopeful heart;
And, when his pitying neighbor sighed for him,
   Thanked God for toil's rough file and sorrow's dart.

And ever in his prayer these words appeared,
   Till rest was gained and joy eternal won,
" O mighty leader of thy chosen race,
   Here, as on high, let all thy will be done ! "

## THE SORROWFUL TEN THOUSAND.

" Few ate any thing that evening, few made fires, and many that night never came to their quarter, but laid themselves down, every man in the place where he happened to be, unable to sleep through sorrow, and a longing for their country, their parents, their wives and children, whom they never expected to see again. In this disposition of mind they all lay down to rest." — *Xenophon's Anabasis.*

ROUND the band of warriors weary,
   Night's star-spangled curtains close;
And, while evening zephyrs whisper,
   Seek the Grecians their repose:
But the sweet, restoring angel,*
   Twin to one we surname " Death,"
Will not near them fold his pinions,
   Woo them with his balmly breath.

Deep within each warrior's bosom
   Was a fount of sacred love,
Welling up for far-off dear ones,
   Faithful as the tender dove.

* " Tired nature's sweet restorer, balmy sleep." — *Young.*

Longed they for their native country,
    As chained eagles to be free;
And they sighed for home's rich blessings,
    As the death-doomed sigh to flee.

With his warrior friends reclining,
    Mused the "Bee of Greece" a while,
Till his dreams took form in action,
    And he rose to bid them smile.
With his eloquence unrivalled,
    Spake to them the "Athenian Muse,"
Till his words the dense clouds lifted,
    And with cheerful hearts they rose.

Then through dangers dire he led them,
    Toward the home they longed to see,
Writing on their banners "Safety,"
    Synonyme of "Victory;"
Till once more, amid their dear ones,
    Sinking swift to calm repose,
They with grateful hearts remembered
    How he cheered their night of woes.

So, while Life's fierce conflicts waging,
    Pausing 'mid the din of strife,
Sleep forsakes our path, and, sighing,
    Long we for a better life,
Then, with eloquence supernal, —
    Ne'er by Xenophon possessed, —
Speaks the world's exemplar Saviour,
    "Come to me and find your rest."

Weary, yearning, fainting spirits,
   Ere in death your eyes shall close,
Follow Him through all earth's dangers:
   He will lead to sweet repose.
As you wave the palms of victory
   On the brighter, better shore,
You will shout, with-grateful spirits,
   "Safe from sin forevermore!"

Not alone for glorious victory
   Over death and grief and pain;
But for safety from the tempter
   Shall you sing with joy again;
And your Leader's wisdom lauding,
   Strike your harp with louder tone,
Singing, "Praise to Jesus ever:
   We are saved through him alone!"

## THE LAST DAY OF WINTER.

[Written on the last day of February.]

HARK! the voice of Boreas shouteth
   From the mountains to the sea,
And the snowy mantle falleth
   From us, brown earth, hiding thee.
Sifting through each tiny crevice,
   Comes the pure, unsullied snow,
Saying, that, with February,
   Stormy winter will not go.

Fast upon the tossing ocean
   Fall the snow-flakes all the day,
Hiding rocky cape and island
   From my wistful gaze that way.
Night comes on; and Frost, the artist,
   Decks my window-pane anew,
Shutting out my friends and neighbors
   From my yet more wishful view.

Boreas shouts! and fast he worketh,
   Heaping up the driven snow,
Till my doorways are blockaded,
   And the paths no foot can know.
By the fire we gladly gather;
   For the poor we breathe a prayer;
Pointing up with Faith's true finger,
   Saying, "There's no winter there!"

God be praised! no cruel winter
   In the land to which we go;
No rude winds so drear and chilling,
   No more friend-dividing snow:
God be praised, while here we linger,
   For the snow, the hail, the rain;
All are parts of his great purpose,
   He will make each riddle plain.

But across the stormy waters,
   In "our home beyond the tide,"
There shall be no dreary winter:
   Love shall in all hearts abide,
Making summer, making music,
   Making joy for earth-worn souls,

While upon the gentle zephyrs
    Sweet the eternal anthem rolls.

Gladly press I onward, upward,
    Cheerful, counting every day,
Welcoming the coming spring-time,
    Making bright mine earthly way;
But beyond it hourly looking
    To the everlasting hills,
Blooming in eternal summer,
    Faith with joy my spirit fills.

Soon for me will close Life's winter,
    Soon the morning glory rise;
Lo! the roseate hue of dawning
    Flushes now the eastern skies.
Soon this earth-life's dreary winter
    I shall recognize no more:
Oh, the bliss of that experience,—
    *Summer on the shining shore!*

## PARTING WORDS.

THOSE parting words! they fell upon our ears
    Like the far sounding of a solemn knell,
And linger now as lingers in the vale
    The sweet-toned echoes of the vesper-bell.

Those parting words! they faded on our ears
    As fade the sunset hues of parting day,
Yet linger in our hearts as still remains
    The holy presence of the twilight ray.

Those parting words! we clasp them to our hearts,
    As clasps a mother her beloved child:
Our memories to each precious sentence cling,
    As child to parent when the storm is wild.

Those parting words remind of yon bright heaven,
    As speaks the sea-shell of the distant main,
Where all who clasped our hand with parting words
    Shall be restored in bliss to us again.

Those parting words shall in our memories sound,
    As sounds for miles Niagara's mighty roar,
And blend their cadence with the welcomes sweet
    Which yet shall greet us from the heavenly shore.

Then sound the pæan song of holy triumph;
    For parting words shall yet in welcomes end,
As morning moonlight and the gleam of stars
    Oft with auroral brightness calmly blend.

## TWILIGHT ON BEVERLY SHORE.

[Written on seeing a picture, by J. A. Suydam, in the Boston Athenæum, entitled "Twilight on the Beverly Shore."]

I HAVE stood on the brow of a cloud-capped hill
    When the god of day passed on,
And have watched with joy while the daylight died,
    And the stars of night were born;

And I love the hour when the eve comes on,
    Though the glory of sunset is o'er:
But few are the twilights so sweet to my soul
    As the twilight on Beverly Shore.

I have rocked on the deep when the billows slept,
    And the shadows of evening fell
O'er the wide, wide waste of the waters blue,
    Where is heard no vesper bell;
And my heart rejoiced in the calm, sweet look
    Which the star-gemmed waves then wore:
But yet not so dear is that long-cherished scene
    As the twilight on Beverly Shore.

'Twas the close of a day when the many chimes,
    And the deep-mouthed cannon's roar,
Had ceased till another "Fourth" should dawn,
    That I stood near the Beverly Shore.
Far off in the shadow the islands rest,
    And the beacon gleams once more,
As Memory presents the sweet scene to my mind
    Of that twilight on Beverly Shore.

Sweet friend, who wert with me in that blissful hour,
    Dear children, then gathered around,
Your presence endeared the bright vision to me,
    And stamped the spot my hallowed ground!
Then gladly I hailed what the artist achieved,
    Preserving that scene evermore,
And welcomed the picture fond Memory could claim,
    As "Twilight on Beverly Shore."

## A PROPHECY.

WITH reverent hand we lift Truth's glorious banner,
    And fealty vow
To all that lifts our sex to power and honor
    In this grand Now

The time has fled when weakness meant but woman:
    The hour has come
When the divine transcends in her the human;
    And 'tis her doom,

Her glorious destiny, to guide this nation
    Far from its sin,
Up to the heights of its serene salvation,
    Its crown to win

Among the people that are known to story
    And classic song.
Then shall no nation be so filled with glory,
    And none so strong,

As this republic, noble, and far-stretching
    From sea to sea;
While its grand influence o'er the waters reaching
    Bids all be free.

Strike, then, the sounding cymbals in this hour!
    Peal forth a blast,
Waking dead nations to the thought of power
    For good to last!

When woman in the state beside her brother
    May nobly toil,
This land shall take a place o'er every other,
    And on its soil

The grandest temple ever reared to Freedom
    In peace shall rise;
Its tower of strength, the truth that all are equal
    Beneath the skies.

And as no bond nor free are known among us
    Since Lincoln wrote;
So neither male nor female shall be counted
    When freemen vote.

God speed the hour when they who've battled bravely
    Shall grandly win,
And women, when the votes here are numbered,
    Be counted in!

Then shall be oped the glorious gates of morning
    For all our race;
And Truth's fair jewel every brow adorning,
    And shall have place

To work for God in working for each other,
    And side by side,
With equal privilege and equal honor,
    In peace t' abide.

We will not faint, then, on this field of freedom,
    But still contend,
With all the power God gives each true reformer,
    Until the end.

And then we'll join the loud and glad hosanna
    The earth shall sing,
When Right and Might enlist beneath one banner,
    And Truth is king.

## BYRON.

BYRON the titled! not of him I sing
    Who wore the coronet with aching brow:
Byron the bard alone my muse inspires;
    His genius only bids my spirit bow.

Impetuous Byron! Like a torrent poured
    His glowing words along the emblazoned page,
As, like an Arab steed o'er desert sands,
    With fiery haste he passed from youth to age.

Alas! that verse like his, which charms the heart,
    And like sweet music fascinates the soul,
The lustre of a snow-white pureness needs,
    The virtuous mind serenely to control.

Byron *the poet* on Parnassus stands,
    His regal brow with early laurels crowned:
Where stands *the man?* Alas, if on Mount Zion
    The soul unprisoned ne'er hath been renowned!

Oh that his heart had bowed, in youth's bright hour
    Or fame-wreathed manhood, to the law divine,
That not alone among the bards of earth
    His laurelled coronet might ever shine!

Too late ? In God's firm hand the scales abide ;
  We leave him to the Judge who cannot err,
But sigh to think the poet we have loved
  Was never *here*, through Christ, a conqueror.

Then, loving, grieving, read " Childe Harold " o'er,
  And trace the footsteps of a royal mind,
And wish that he in Christian faith had bowed,
  And known the luxury of a will resigned.

1864.

## THE PALACE AND THE ANGEL.

[Read at a meeting of the " Social Readers," Nov. 28, 1864.]

WE, " Social Readers," meet to-night,
  As we are wont to meet,
Nor to the magic circle came
  With slow, unwilling feet ;
For we have learned to love the band
Who pledge to wisdom heart and hand.

To greet our president * we all
  With right good will have come,
And wish her every joy within
  Her new and pleasant home :
Here may she peace and plenty know !
Here may her soul in wisdom grow !

* Miss Emily Ruggles.

Now let me tell in simple words
   A dream I had to-day.
True visions come at midnight hours;
   But waking dreams, they say,
May be enjoyed at any time,
And oft a record find in rhyme.

I saw a mansion, fairer e'en
   Than this where we have met:
An angel with serenest air
   Gave welcome at the gate;
And soft and low he whispered, "See,
God has been guiding thee to me!"

I entered at the door; and lo!
   Before my gladdened eyes
Appeared the forms of valued friends,
   (I gazed in sweet surprise!)
The "Social Readers" all were there,
As now the band is gathered here.

And some were there I never knew, —
   Some wisdom-loving souls
Who left our circle long ago,
   And, where Life's river rolls,
Had waited for our lingering feet
To echo on the golden street.

They gathered round me as I stood
   Anear my angel-guide,
And welcomed me, to learn with them
   The lessons we had tried
In vain to study while on earth,
Where wisdom-longings had their birth.

On every brow a radiant star
   Shone in that wondrous hour:
My spirit felt a holier joy
   Than e'er it knew before;
And from my eyes a veil seemed drawn,
As the kind angel led us on.

From room to room the angel passed;
   We followed, learning still.
Smiles told how willingly we all
   Obeyed the angel's will.
And soon we learned the angel's name:
'Twas "Progress;" and from God he came.

So we in Wisdom's palace dwelt
   With happy hearts the while,
And sipped the nectar only found
   On earth by weary toil.
All gladly by the angel fed,
And strengthened by the heavenly bread.

I woke: and, as a bubble bright
   With brilliant rainbow hues,
My vision fled, but memory caught
   Some fragments; and I muse
To-night on what the dream hath taught,
Which seemed with joy prophetic fraught.

One lesson only now I tell:
   This,— that there comes a day
When all who wisdom truly seek
   Will enter wisdom's way,
And at her palace-gate will stand,
   And take that angel's welcome hand.

## THE GRECIAN ATHLETE.

WHEN ancient heroes sought to win
   The green Olympic crown,
And in the races victors prove,
   And gain a high renown,
With self-denial they shunned excess,
   O temperance divine!
That worthily around their brows
   The civic wreath might twine.

And should not we who seek a prize
   Far higher than they sought,
Who seek a crown more fair than those
   By human fingers wrought,
Be willing to forego the cup,
   Its doubtful joys to shun,
That we may hear our umpire say,
   "Hero, thou hast well done!"

Ah, yes! immortal bliss we seek,
   A diadem on high;
And pressing onward in the race,
   And looking toward the sky,
Each earthly weight we lay aside,
   Besetting sins ignore,
Heed not the wine-cup's fatal charm,
   And sip its sweets no mo.

Then shall our names, as heroes true,
   Angel recorded stand;
Then shall the fadeless crown be won,
   And worn at God's right hand.

From all the victor host shall sound
   Triumphant shouts abroad,
And praise for conquering grace be given
   Forever to the Lord.

## THE RIDE.

LOW hung the leaden clouds o'er Reading paths;
   The damp breath of the salt east wind was chill;
And far from spring-like seemed the cheerless day,
   While sad its influence on the heart and will.

There came an hour when rifted clouds proclaimed
   That still the sun above them brightly shone:
Then came thy message, and with happier heart
   I sped with thee o'er paths before unknown.

Along the country roads we quietly ride,
   And watch the tokens of Spring's gentle reign:
The feathery catkins of the roadside trees
   In graceful beauty meet our eyes again.

The bending willows now are clothed in green;
   Red flowerets on the maples we behold;
Lo! promise-blossoms deck the cherries too,
   And emerald meadows oft are starred with gold.

I see the birds flit from the half-clad trees,
   To evergreens where summer beauty shines;
And hear their welcome, spring-time carol sweet,
   Far off and high, amid the lofty pines.

Aye, spring has come, although the days are dark
  With lowering clouds, and chill the east winds
      blow:
Lo! still the promise is to man fulfilled,
  Seed-time and harvest all the earth shall know.

How is it with thee, O my soul! to-day?
  God grant the seeds of holy truth are thine,
To grow in beauty through Life's changeful spring,
  And ripen for the harvest-field divine.

## CHRISTMAS EVE.

IT was Christmas Eve, and the stars shone bright,
  But the Frost-King reigned around;
And the flakes which fell so soft and light
  Still lay on the frozen ground.

I walked the street of an ancient town;
  And a spirit walked with me:
I saw on the noble brow no frown;
  And I whispered, "A welcome to thee."

He gave me a mirror which showed the Past, —
  'Twas the Future I longed to know,
Till he said, with a voice like the wintry blast,
  All chilling, severe, "Not so!"

Then I meekly said, "In the Lord's own time;"
  And I gazed in the magic glass;
And I saw a vision sweet, sublime,
  With its glorious angels, pass.

Then he bade me list; and the air was stirred
  By a sweeter than mortal tone:
'Twas the song of the host the shepherds heard
  When the Star of Bethlehem shone.

And my heart beat high with a hope to join
  In that everlasting song;
And I asked of him in whose hand was mine,
  "How long must I wait? — how long?"

"Sing it now, with a thankful heart, — sing it now:
  Let thy life be a Christmas glee!"
And a kiss of peace felt my upturned brow,
  From the spirit that walked with me.

Then he passed away from that quiet path,
  With adieu like the zephyr's sigh;
And my soul rejoiced in the hope that earth
  Would yet echo the song of the sky.

## "WE ALL DO FADE AS A LEAF."

THROUGH forest-paths we love,
  'Mid autumn-colored foliage, to stray;
Yet fallen leaves, which rustle as we move,
  There whisper of decay.

Upon the billowy deep
  We gladly watch the lovely moonlight sheen, —
A line of silver where the blue waves sleep, —
  Till clouds obscure the scene.

With rapture-speaking eye,
   We gaze upon each amber-tinted cloud
Which decorates the occidental sky,
   Ere night shall earth enshroud.

And gladly oft we tread
   The flower-decked garden paths with cherished friend,
Gathering rare blossoms for the queenly head,
   Rich fragrance there to spend.

But change comes o'er each scene;
   And leaves and flowerets wither and decay.
Some lesson Nature thus would teach, I ween,—
   Some warning thus convey.

Hark! from the prophet-page
   Which points the path of duty to each soul,
And tells the destiny of fool and sage,
   To us the tidings roll.

Like autumn leaves *we* fade,
   Like sunset glory from the gorgeous west,
Like moonlight beauty when night's queen is hid,
   Like flowers once gayly drest.

'Tis well! I meekly bow,
   O King of kings! to this thy high behest:
Time writes too many wrinkles on my brow
   For me to doubt the rest.

I know that I must die.
   Like withered leaf by chill autumnal blast,
Swept from the parent-stem, I, too, must lie
   Where all shall lie at last.

Though long grass soon may wave
  Upon the turf 'neath which my form may rest,
And loving, loved ones weep above my grave,
  I welcome thy behest.

Where everlasting Spring
  With fadeless blossoms decks the verdant plain,
Where ransomed souls eternal praises sing,
  There shall I live again.

We fade; but thanks to Thee,
  O Jesus! who hath conquered death and sin,
We only fade to brighten, die to be
  Where Death no prize can win.

## THE BOOK OF JOB.

BRING the volume best and eldest;
  Read that record, so sublime,
Of the man with wondrous patience,
  Hero on the field of Time.

Read each grand, each noble sentence,
  Touched by true poetic fire;
He who would imbibe its spirit
  Hath upon his banner, " Higher.

When the storm-clouds thickly gather
  O'er thy thorny, pilgrim way,
Trust, like Job, till gleam the rainbows,
  Till the night is turned to day.

Trust that Friend, the best, the truest,
　Who will never leave thy side,
If in storms or in the sunshine
　Thou in patience wilt abide.

Dark sometimes must be our pathway,
　Clouds will gather overhead,
And our fondly loved and cherished
　Oft be numbered with the dead.

But in God the Christian trusting
　Can the song of triumph sing.
O'er him hath the grave no victory,
　Death for him can have no sting.

Wrap the mantle, then, of patience,
　Round thy spirit, suffering one:
Perfect through thine earthly sorrow,
　Christ shall claim thee as his own.

Calmly on thy Saviour leaning,
　Through the tearful valley go,
Soon the mount of bliss ascending,
　Losing thought of earthly woe.

## THE POWER OF THE BEAUTIFUL.

THE time of singing birds is here;
　The annual miracle's begun;
And those who tread the forest-paths
　Can pluck the blossoms, one by one.

It minds me of a story told,
  Concerning flowers bright and fair,
Which, blooming near a cottage doomed,
  Were yet as silent guardians there.

One day, while War's rude, crushing tread
  Was heard o'er Southern plains afar,
While hearts were rendered desolate,
  Homes, too, oft met the fate of war,
With swift revenge the soldiery
  To many a cot the torch applied,
Until at last to one they came,
  With sweet, bright flowerets at its side.

Their beauty was so eloquent,
  The cottage, flower-adorned, was spared,
As if an angel interposed
  When man the sword of vengeance bared.
Thus hath the Beautiful o'er man
  A wondrous and a holy power;
Thus can it soothe the wrathful waves
  That rise in Passion's stormy hour.

O Thou who cloth'st each blade of grass,
  And paint'st the petals of the rose,
And fill'st the earth with beauty rare,
  To us thy character disclose,
Till every beauteous thing of earth
  Shall whisper to our souls of heaven;
And thine own beauty, holiness,
  Shall be to all our spirits given!

## MOONLIGHT ON THE OCEAN.

'TIS moonlight on the ocean; and the mighty waters sleep,
Save where the line of radiance comes across the pathless deep:
There billows weave a fairy dance, and sparkle in the light
Which falls so softly on them now, amid the hush of night.

I stand upon the hill-top green, and gaze far o'er the main,
And see the rocky islets\* there, and hear the waves again,
Which beat in gentle cadences upon the pebbly shore,
And 'mind me of a distant islet† my eyes may see no more.

Home, home, beyond those waters! O home so dear to me!
Not e'en the crested billows can divide my heart from thee.
Are moonbeams resting on the waves which break along thy shore?
And do the eyes I long to greet gaze on them as before?

\* Lowell Island, &c.     † Nantucket.

Moonlight upon the ocean: oh! there is no fairer scene
This side the pearly gates of heaven, for mortal eyes, I ween;
And, while I gaze, my heart ascends with grateful praise to Him
Before whose beauteous holiness the sheen of earth grows dim.

Father and Saviour! Spirit pure! my heart ascends to thee,
That, wheresoe'er upon this earth my weary feet may be,
My eyes may gaze on scenes so fair through Faith's revealing glass,
That trustfully toward future days my steps may onward pass.

For he who sends the moonlight now to make the deep so fair —
God's smile upon the waters dark when gloomy night is there —
Can send his Spirit's joyful light to gleam along my way, —
A line of holy radiance and a part of heaven's day.

O God! I thank thee for the hours, when, standing by the sea,
Alone, or with beloved friends, my heart is drawn to thee;
For, while its quiet loveliness my spirit doth control,
This moonlight on the ocean shall be sunlight in my soul.

## A TRIBUTE OF GRATITUDE.

[Respectfully inscribed to Mrs. B. Wallis, Jun., author of "Life in Feejee."]

MY God, I thank thee! to thy lofty throne
    In gratitude I lift my heart to-night;
For every good and perfect gift comes down
    From thee, as from the sun its rays of light.

Each graceful-formed and lovely-tinted flower
    Which decks the earth, as stars the evening sky,
Is emblematic of thy love and power,
    And speaks of heaven, where flowerets never die.

Such hast thou sent me by the hand of one
    United to me by the mystic tie
Which binds in union sweet who seek alone
    Thy will to do, who reignest e'er on high.

By her fair flowers thou this day hast sent,
    Awaking memories of an island shore,
While tears and smiles within my heart were blent,
    At thought of gardens I may tread no more.

Yet, Father, still I thank thee; for I read
    On every petal, as a holy page,
That thou art here, thou knowest my spirit-need,
    And wilt that spirit's grief by love assuage.

Then, as the token that warm hearts are here,
    And loving souls are still around my way,
I take them. Father, this petition hear:
    Oh guide the giver to thy perfect day!

## THE BOYS' HYMN.

[Toplady's beautiful hymn, "Rock of Ages, cleft for me," was finely sung by the boys on board the School Ship "Massachusetts," then in Beverly Harbor, sabbath afternoon, Sept. 7, 1862, at the close of services held on board by Rev. Dr. Jos. Abbott and Rev. J. C. Foster. It is related of the late Prince Albert, that he repeated in his last hours this comforting hymn; and the remembrance of this fact, while the lads were singing, suggested the following lines:—]

THE sabbath hours were almost spent,
   The sun was in the west,
When, gently rocking with the tide
   Upon old ocean's breast,
I listened to a sacred song,
   Whose utterance thrilled mine heart,
And, where its echoes floated, stood
   Reluctant to depart.

They sang,—those boys,—in sweetest tones,
   Of Christ, the smitten Rock:
I thought of England's mourning queen,
   When first she knew the shock
Of widowhood, and how her heart
   Sweet comfort must have known,
Since Albert told in that sweet hymn
   He trusted Christ alone.

The meeting closed, the daylight waned;
   We bade the ship adieu;
And, gliding o'er the moon-lit waves,
   To shore we quickly drew:

But long within our memories
   That evening hour will dwell, —
The rising moon, the silvered waves,
   And day's serene farewell.

And blending with the thought of words
   In kindness spoken there,
And with the hymns by others sung,
   And with the voice of prayer,
Will come the sound of music sweet, —
   The hymn the young lads sung
About the sheltering, smitten Rock
   To which Prince Albert clung.

O Rock of Ages! in thy side
   Sweet refuge may we know,
When gathering storms our skies obscure,
   And wintry winds may blow!
And may the youthful band which sang
   That loved and precious hymn,
By grace be fitted for the choir
   Of holy seraphim!

## GLORY TO GOD ALONE!

"GLORY to God alone!" aloud they cry
   Who bow before the throne;
And answering praises fill the world on high,
   "Glory to God alone!"

When Israel from the land of bondage came,
    Thine arm was their defence;
And thine the pillar of the cloud and flame,
    To lead thy people thence.

Thou, when Life's hosts on tossing waves were driven,
    Didst light fair Bethlehem's star,
To guide the wanderer to the port of heaven,
    From sin and sorrow far.

Still shines the star of hope above Life's waves;
    Thy flock thou still dost lead;
Thine arm is mighty yet thine own to save,
    And thou our souls doth feed.

Then loud along the vaulted arch above,
    Thy praises should resound;
And prayer to Thee, — God of eternal love! —
    "Make earth all hallowed ground!"

Thine is the work: let thine the glory be
    Who brought salvation down:
O Jesus! Master! praise belongs to thee,
    And thou must wear the crown.

Thou Lamb of God! while saints and angels sing,
    Sit thou upon thy throne:
Then henceforth let the heavenly chorus ring,
    "Glory to God alone!"

## "INSULA BONÆ FORTUNÆ."

NOT here the spicy breezes float,
    Nor palms luxuriant wave,
Nor brilliant birds with curious note
    In sparkling fountains lave ;
For this is not Sumatra's isle,*
Upon which rests Good Fortune's smile.

But here the cool sea-breezes blow
    Through summer's sunny hours,
And Health's glad angels come and go,
    With soothing, magic powers;
And to the invalid it seems
The " Fortune Island " of his dreams.

Away from care, away from toil,
    The wanderer here may rest,
And find upon his native soil
    The joys he loves the best :
Sweet converse with each long-loved friend,
And peace in God that knows no end.

To me this isle is doubly dear,
    Because my birth-place twice : †

---

\* The ancients were accustomed to call Sumatra "Insula Bonæ Fortunæ," or the "Island of Good Fortune."

† It is related of the youthful, godly Summerfield, that, on his arrival in this country, he was asked by a doctor of divinity the place of his nativity. He mentioned both Liverpool and Dublin. "How can that be?" inquired the D.D. Summerfield turned, and, fixing on his interrogator a penetrating gaze, answered with solemn emphasis, in the words of Christ to Nicodemus, "Art thou a master in Israel, and knowest not these things?"

The tender Shepherd found me here,
  And bade me know his voice.
Ah! then this " island of the sea "
Hath been Good Fortune's isle to me.

God bless our sea-beat island home!
  Where Freedom early found
A refuge from an unjust doom *
  Is surely hallowed ground.
And, reader, may it prove to thee,
" Insula Bonæ Fortunæ "!

## ROUND HILL.

[Suggested by a recent visit to a hill of this name in Saugus, in company with the Essex Institute.]

BRIGHT was the morning hour when erst we pressed
  That sunny hill-top with our stranger feet,
And viewed with joy the rural beauty round,
  And the blue waves where earth and heaven meet.

Nearer, the river, with its gentle flow,
  Winding in serpent folds its azure way,
And farther, in the orient horizon,
  Old ocean sparkling 'neath the orb of day,

---

* Some of the earliest settlers of Nantucket came here to find a refuge from penalties incurred by righteous disobedience to the unjust laws which forbade kindness to Quakers.

Both emblems of the truth we humbly seek :
    Here a small streamlet with a sinuous course ;
There the broad sea of wisdom infinite,
    Where we may bathe when Life shall reach its source.

Round Hill ! thy name is all unknown to fame ;
    Historic pages mention not of thee ;
Yet Memory oft shall view thy grassy top,
    Crowned with its single, fence-encircled tree.

That tree spoke to my soul of one afar, —
    A tree beneath whose shadow lies the dust
Of one endeared to Christians o'er the earth,*
    Now crowned and sanctified amid the just.

The hopia-tree ! which stands alone and far
    Where the swift waters of the Salwen flow,
And mingle in the distance with the waves
    Whereon the barks of India come and go.

Rivers and oceans in the pictures blend,
    Hilltops and lonely trees; but, thanks to God !
*That* is a tree upon a heathen soil,
    *This* a fair elm in thine own land, O Lord !

Thy land ! oh, make it thine yet more and more !
    While blood baptizes oft the sacred soil ;
And when the shout of " Peace ! " shall echo wide,
    Let Freedom bloom in beauty 'neath thy smile.

Then on this hilltop of the pilgrim shore
    May the bright banner of our country wave,
A token that the storm at last is o'er,
    And God's bright rainbow gleams for every slave !

    * Mrs. Ann H. Judson.

## THE LOVE-FEAST.

[Suggested by attending a religious meeting with this designation, held in the Methodist Chapel, Centre Street, Nantucket, June 17, 1860.]

They met in His name who to each loving heart
    The life-giving word had once spoken;
The flow of whose peace in full many a soul
    For long years had continued unbroken.

They met in His name, to renew every vow
    Of love, and of earnest devotion
To God and his cause, till the hearts of all men
    Are his own, on the land and the ocean.

They met; and the tide of their faith rose high,
    As the songs of Zion sounded,
And ebbed no more through that evening hour,
    For their love to God abounded.

They met; and my heart beat high with joy
    To meet with those dear believers;
And my thoughts went forward to the mansions fair,
    Which are waiting to receive us.

O rapturous thought! that no tears shall fall
    When the ransomed meet in heaven:
E'en penitent grief shall be changed to joy,
    Where the crown of live is given.

No faltering tongue shall His praise declare,
   In that meeting of saints in glory;
For the love-feast of the Lamb shall hear
   Each member tell one story.

A tale of triumph, of victory won
   Through the might of the conquering Saviour, —
Of love unmixed from a purified heart,
   "Made perfect in love" forever.

God grant us a home with that glorified throng
   Who the love of our Lord are recounting,
Who from glory to glory, from grace unto grace,
   For ever and ever are mounting!

## "UPS AND DOWNS."

THIS life is all a battle-field;
   And Right and Wrong are waging
A mighty warfare in the earth,
   In which we're all engaging.

Then gird the Christian armor on,
   And bravely forth to strife:
There's nothing like the Christian's hope,
   For the "ups and downs" of life.

Life hath its gulf-streams, and too oft
   Its maelstroms of temptation:
He's safe alone whose pilot is
   The Captain of Salvation.

And Life is full of changeful scenes,
  While joy and sorrow pass,
Like waves of shadow chasing swift
  O'er long, green summer grass.

Then seek the guidance of that star
  Which shines where strife's suspended:
There rest and joy the victor wait;
  There " ups and downs " are ended,

Yes, gird the Christian armor on,
  And bravely forth to strife:
There's nothing like the Christian's hope
  For the " ups and downs " of life.

---

## GOD REIGNS.

[Read at the Essex County Good Templars' Union, held in Beverly, May 3, 1865.]

HARK to the minstrel monarch's lifted voice,
  Down the long ages borne to distant ears,
" Jehovah reigneth, let the earth rejoice ! "
  And quelled forever be our rising fears.

God reigns ! our land, of every land the best,
  Has long been darkened by the cloud of war;
And on the shore of public peace and joy
  Break the huge billows with tumultuous roar.

Yet high o'er every surge the mighty God,
  Throned as of old, doth still the sceptre wield:
He parts the crimson waves with lifted rod,
  And lo! the long-sought Canaan stands revealed.

But in our joy, as we beheld the dawn
  Of the bright era when fair Peace shall reign,
The bold assassin turned our night to morn,
  And sorrow wraps our war-cursed land again.

Why is it thus? we ask, but ask in vain:
  Enough, that high o'er earth and earthly things
The Lord our God, our *Father*, still doth reign;
  Still is he Lord of lords, and King of kings.

In him we'll trust whatever may befall,
  Assured that love and wisdom cannot err:
No strange event shall our strong souls appall,
  For God at last must be the conqueror.

Yes, Wrong shall die, and Truth supreme shall reign;
  And we who toil in this divine reform
Are not on board the temperance ship in vain,
  But safe shall outride each impending storm;

And see the drunkard rescued from his woe,
  The wine-cup banished from the social band,
The paths made pure where youthful steps must go,
  And all intemperance banished from the land.

Strong be our faith in this, — that, while we toil,
  God watches o'er us to reward our pains:
Seed sown in tears shall spring forth from the soil,
  And give us golden harvests; for God reigns!

## RETURN OF THE JEWS TO PALESTINE.

" The Sultan of Turkey is encouraging Jewish emigration to Palestine, and is offering to sell them as much land as they choose to buy; and it is said has even expressed a willingness to dispose of the Mosque of Omar to them, which it will be recollected stands upon the very site of the Jewish Temple on Mount Moriah. . . . Some of the hills around Jerusalem have already become Jewish property; and it is by no means improbable that some of the present generation will see the entire city of Jerusalem again in the hands of its ancient owners. That mighty revolutions will follow in the wake of such an event is probably as certain as that the Jews will return at all; at all events, affairs in that immediate region of the East must ere long become an engrossing theme among the nations of the earth." — *Phil. Press.*

THEY come! to Olive's brow they come!
    The scattered tribes return!
They gaze on dear Jerusalem,
    O'er which their spirits yearn.
O wondrous page of history!
    O prophecy o'erpast!
For Jewish feet shall tread the courts
    Of Omar's mosque at last.

Where are the barriers, firm and strong,
    To check the advancing tide?
Where are the Roman soldiers now?
    Where is the Moslem pride?
God speaks: t'is done! Those prophet-tones
    Which through the ages rang
No longer sound in Jewish ears
    With heavy, martial clang.

The angel-song o'er Bethlehem's plains —
    The note of peace and love —
Now like Creation's fiat sounds,
    And all the world shall move.

On Europe's plains, 'neath Syria's palms,
  May sanguine currents flow;
Yet louder sounds the anthem sweet
  Which all the world shall know.

E'en 'though to War's fell power, alas!
  Broad lands may still be given,
Yet " Peace on earth, good will to men,
  Glory to God in heaven,"
Shall soon the song of nations be, —
  Our own and all beside, —
Till the glad stream of brotherhood
  Flows a resistless tide.

Partition walls shall crumble then,
  And Jew and Gentile bend,
With loving hearts, at one fair shrine,
  Their offerings to blend.
Then shall the bondman fling his chains
  With joyful shout away;
And every heart with praise shall hail
  Earth's bright millennial day.

---

## THE MOONLIGHT SCENE.

[Suggested by a picture of George Southward's, representing a river-view in the summer moonlight.]

HOW beautiful! the moonlight falls
  So softly o'er the wave,
It minds me of the land whose shore
  God's boundless love doth lave.

How gloriously the moonbeams dance
   Upon the summer sea,
As if a fairy festival
   Was held in merry glee!

How true to Nature! Launch the boat
   O ye upon the shore!
And gently on that sparkling tide
   Now ply the dripping oar.

Would I were there, and by my side
   Some noble, cherished friend,
Glad hours upon those moonlit waves
   Alone with me to spend!

The soothing charm of such a scene!
   It cometh o'er my soul,
And, with a welcome glad and free,
   I bow to its control.

O Thou who giveth man the power
   Thy fair works thus to show!
Thanks for the boon, as now my soul
   The blessedness may know

Of gazing on a scene like this,
   Which minds me of that land
Where all is beautiful and bright,
   Or glorious and grand.

## THEY MARRY NOT IN HEAVEN.

"In the resurrection they neither marry, nor are given in marriage, but are as the angels of God in heaven." — MATT. xxii. 30.

THEY marry not in heaven!
   Love is not bartered there for sordid gold,
Nor youth's bright hopes nor beauty's charms are sold;
      But love alone is given
For its equivalent, and "love for love"
Is all the merchant-rule of those above.

      They marry not in heaven!
The Mussulman can claim no "houri" there.
Women with souls the Christian's heaven share,
      And every bond is riven
Which mars the freedom of the holy soul,
And gives to sense and sin a sad control.

      They marry not in heaven!
And yet those earth-born ties, if true and fond,
Uniting spirits in the *true* marriage-bond,
      Will not be sadly riven:
They who were one on earth henceforth shall rove
Still wedded lovers in the world above.

      They marry not in heaven!
But they who, wandering like the dove, alone,
No rest with fond, true mate on earth have known;
      And nobly here have striven

The yearnings of the soul to satisfy,
By toiling, though alone, with purpose high, —

*They* marry not in heaven;
But they shall find, amid the shining throng,
Some kindred souls to echo back their song,
Some harps whose strings have given
No answering notes on earth to human love,
Waiting to meet them in that world above.

They marry not in heaven!
And yet in that celestial, glorious home,
Heart bound to heart, and hand in hand, they roam
To whom on earth was given
A union sweet of hearts, though not of hands,
A blending which each seraph understands.

They marry not in heaven!
But all the joy which glowing fancy paints,
The gift of God, the heritage of saints,
To ransomed souls is given,
Where kindred spirits meet to part no more,
And blend, like rivers, on Life's farther shore.

They marry not in heaven!
O God of love! whose wise and holy plan
Of human wedlock oft is marred by man,
Praise to thy name be given!
That loving souls shall find communion sweet,
And free from sin, where all thy children meet.

## REST FOR THE TRUE LABORER.

THERE'S a world of light and beauty
   For the friends of right and duty;
  There shall all the weary rest,
  There the sorrowing shall be blest.
In that land of joy and gladness,
Where no spirit dreams of sadness,
  Smiles illumine every brow,
  As before the throne they bow.

Those on earth who follow Jesus,
And in heaven place their treasures,
  There shall find a harp and crown,
  When earth's weapons are laid down.
They who seek, as souls immortal,
Entrance through the starry portal,
  Safe from every earthly woe,
  Tears and sighs no more shall know.

They whose souls are often weary,
And to whom earth's path seems dreary,
  As they daily, nightly toil,
  Plough the sea, or till the soil;
All who seek, by earnest labor,
Highest good of self and neighbor,
  All who toil aright, shall rest
  Where the ransomed soul is blest.

## THE SHIPWRECK.

DAYLIGHT was fading o'er the billowy deep;
   A noble ship approached the wished-for shore;
And watching eyes, which often used to weep
   For distant friends, now hope to weep no more.

A few hours only, and they hope to moor
   Their bark beside the land they love so well, —
To hear fond welcomes from that longed-for shore,
   Sweeter than music-tones or vesper-bell.

As from the west the rose-tint faded fast,
   The stars hung out their banners in the sky,
The lighthouse gleamed afar, the evening blast
   Sank to a zephyr like a lover's sigh.

With throbbing hearts the waiting ones reposed,
   To gather strength for joys with coming day;
Yet scarce their eyelids with sweet slumber closed,
   Ere they were wakened by the dash of spray.

And by the sudden shock which told a tale
   Of ocean shipwreck and its horrors dire:
For them in vain, though hushed the stormy gale,
   Now gleamed across the deep the beacon-fire.

The boats were crowded till they held no more,
   And frantic cries arose from many there, —
That, though the night was calm, the distant shore
   And all its blessings they could never share.

Ah, why this sad close of a voyage so near
  Its happiest end upon the destined shore!
Oh! had the wine-cup never sparkled there,
  No death-cry would have blent with ocean's roar.

## MRS. HEMANS ON THE SEA-SHORE.

"The sea-shore was her Forest of Ardennes, and she loved it for its loneliness and freedom well. It was a favorite freak of hers, when quite a child, to get up privately, after careful attendants had fancied her safe in bed, and making her way down to the water side, to indulge herself with a stolen bath." — *Henry E. Chorley's Memorials of Mrs. Hemans.*

ALONE and by the ocean's side,
  Night's sober mantle cast around,
Afar from haunts of wealth and pride,
  The solitude she sought was found.

And who, save those who feel as she,
  Can tell the joys that filled her soul,
As, vast and fathomless and free,
  She saw the mighty billows roll?

Perchance upon her spirit's shrine
  There burned afresh poetic fire,
As there she mused on things divine,
  Or sounded there her sweet-toned lyre.

The visions of her early youth,
  Beside the lonely, heaving main,
Oh! were they not love, hope, and truth,
  In after-life recalled again?

How oft the scenes in early life
    Of future days a type appears!
Then knew not Hemans' soul the strife,
    The joys and griefs, of after years!

No more she seeks that lonely shore
    For whom Castalian waters flowed;
No more on earth she treads the path
    Which leads to heaven's bright abode.

Forever o'er are all her cares,
    Her sorrows, and her earthly joys;
For praises now are changed her prayers,
    And heaven's own work her mind employs.

## WENHAM-LAKE ICE.

[An American travelling in England, a few years ago, noticed in a London street the advertisement, "Wenham-Lake Ice!" His thoughts are supposed to be uttered in the following lines: —]

FAR from my home upon New-England shores,
    Where Pilgrim feet the rocks have sanctified,
I tread Old England's crowded streets, alone
    In the thronged capital, her boast and pride.

All day, for many a day, my thoughts have been
    In the historic Past, and in the Tower,
Or in the Abbey where Fame's children lie, —
    My heart has been with England every hour.

But now a rush of memories sad and sweet
    Comes to my mind, as, gazing, in a trice
My spirit leaps at a familiar name:
    There's magic in those words, "Lake-Wenham Ice!"

I seem to see that placid, silvery sheet
    Spread out beneath the moonbeams far away,
Or hear its mimic billows kiss the shore
    As there I linger at the close of day.

Far off! — three thousand miles of salt sea lie
    Between me and thy waters fresh and clear:
I may not taste the nectar from thee quaffed,
    Nor bathe in thee again for many a year.

Yet even here thy virtues may be known:
    Thou hast a magic for the stranger too;
Thy *name* awakes sweet music in *my* soul,
    Thy *self*, congealed, may soothe a *stranger's* woe.

Where the worn sufferer, with the throbbing pulse,
    Awaits Death's mandate, thou may'st haply go;
Lay thy cool fingers gently on his brow,
    Till the blood cometh evenly and slow.

So, like the fabled fountain, thou shalt be
    The "*aqua vitæ*" for the stranger's hand
That dips with faith the chalice in thy wave,
    Wafted by commerce to our mother-land.

Lake Wenham! on thy shore I hope to stand,
    And gaze again across thy waters blue,
And in that fairer than each foreign land,
    Beneath the Stars and Stripes, thy beauty view.

## RALLY FOR TEMPERANCE.

[Read at a meeting of Mystic Lodge, Feb. 1, 1865.]

WE rally round the flag, my friends,
    We rally here to-night,
Unconquered and unshrinking still,
    Strong for the True and Right.
Our banner flutters in the breeze,
    The good old temperance flag:
We will not crush its ample folds,
    We lower it to no rag.

E'en as our country's " dear old flag "
    Waves far o'er vale and hill ;
So shall the temperance banner wave,
    The pledge of triumph still.
The young are pressing to our ranks,
    With temperance youth to crown ;
And they will bear their banner high,
    When we must lay it down.

The day of freedom will at length
    For each inebriate dawn,
As gloweth for the bondman now,
    Beneath our flag, the morn.
Oh, not in word let us alone
    The friends of temperance be !
But let us labor, — strike the axe
    At every cumbering tree.

In word and deed, in heart and soul,
    To temperance ever true,
Let us our appetites control,
    And win companions too.
So shall our order stronger be,
    Our lodge a type more true
Of that high temple where He sits
    Whose face we hope to view.

There, in the grandest lodge of all,
    Where angel anthems sound,
May we all gather when our work
    No more on earth is found!
All have the Chief's high welcome then,
    All speak the password sweet,
And clasp the friendly hand anew
    Where all *Good* Templars meet!

## TO ONE WHO HAS LENT ME THE WORKS OF SWEDENBORG.

As when the fainting traveller meets upon the desert sands
With one whose stranger heart is kind and his need understands,
Though lips all parched may not express the thirsty traveller's joy,
Yet beams the gratitude he feels forth from his speaking eye.

So I to thee can scarce describe, in simple rhymes like mine,
The grateful fount within my soul which welleth up to thine;
Yet I will strive to *look* my joy by living as *he* taught
Whose volumes of divinest lore thou to my view hast brought.

Long have I sighed to ponder o'er the pages of the sage
Whose revelations give to youth the wisdom of old age;
Who teaches that *enjoyment may*, yet never *must* be ours,
But "*Duty!*" is the rallying cry which calls to *use* our powers.

Not for our selfish joy alone the paths of earth we tread;
But while the angels guard our steps, God watching overhead,
We are to seek man's highest good by usefulness and love,
Assured that all who labor here have sweeter rest above.

What if our paths sometimes are strewn with thorns so sharp and hard,
We almost cease to hope for paths along a smooth green sward!
God's eye is on us; and his love, his providence divine,
Is polishing our spirits then, that we as gems may shine

In that fair land of use and love, of peace and pure
    delight,
Which burst upon the northern seer's enraptured
    spirit's sight:
There shall the sufferer for truth be crowned with
    fadeless joy,
And in the works his heart hath loved find evermore
    employ.

To thee, O God! our spirit's guide to all sublime and
    pure,
Be rendered praise for giving man such lofty, won-
    drous lore,
His heart to strengthen, soul to cheer, along Life's pil-
    grim way,
And ope to him, in sorrow's night, some glimpses of
    the day.

Then next to thee, kind friend, my thanks forever
    shall be given,
Since thou hast helped me thus to draw yet nearer
    to that heaven
Where through the circling ages may thy ransomed
    spirit dwell,
And I be gifted then with power my gratitude to tell!

God bless thee, guide thee, crown thee his, when
    mortal life is o'er,
And give us blissful meetings oft upon the shining
    shore,
Where with angelic wisdom we his providence may
    see,
My footsteps from an island shore directing here to
    thee.

## GOD AND LITTLE CHILDREN.

"I love God and little children." — JEAN PAUL RICHTER.

THE flowers of the field, and the gems of the mine,
　The pearls of the deep, and the stars in the sky,
May be brilliant and beauteous, but not so divine
　As the dear little children, born never to die.
God's hand we behold in the tints blossoms wear,
　As they deck earth with beauty, and gladden our eyes;
But nor star-spangled midnight, nor flowers may declare,
　So well as dear children, our God in the skies.

He knew this who blessed them, and said, "Evermore,
　Oh suffer the children to come unto me!"
For the glorified host on eternity's shore
　Are like little children in innocency.
In heaven their angels forever behold
　His face whose bright glory no prophet could bear:
That heart, like a glacier, must ever be cold,
　Who could wish for a heaven no infant could share.

We love them who gather among them to-day,
　And greet their gay banners and faces so bright;
Rejoicing that none need to falter or stray
　In their path through this world to the region of light.

We celebrate now an historic event,* —
   Here first children gathered, a sabbath-school
      band : †
We proudly rejoice that from this village went
   A voice for the sabbath school through our fair
      land.

The women, God-honored! who gathered them first
   In the school of the sabbath, to learn of its Lord,
Saw the bud of bright promise to full beauty burst,
   And then "went up higher" to take their reward.
Be their memory still cherished while children are
      found
   Life's alphabet conning in innocent glee!
May their spirit of faithfulness ever abound
   With all who the teachers of children may be!

This day a new motto we'll take as our own, —
   "Little children and God!" "Little children and
      God!"
And pray that our pathways on earth may be known
   By the flowers that we plant along infancy's road.
And then, when our toil in this life shall be o'er, —
   All our labors in sabbath school faithfully done, —
Life-crowned and rejoicing, we'll sing evermore,
   "All praise to the Saviour through whom we have
      won."

---

\* Semi-centennial celebration of opening of sabbath school in Beverly.
† The first sabbath school in Beverly, and in the country it is said, was established in 1810, by Hannah Hill and Joanna B. Prince.

## THE MIDNIGHT MEETING.*

'TWAS ten at night; and I, with weary feet,
My steps turned toward a new and blest retreat,
Where sin-cursed womanhood might find a friend,
And sinful man a kind and helping hand, —
Where those who homeless walked the midnight round
A home and a Redeemer too had found.
  My heart rejoiced then with a gospel faith
In the great fatherhood of One who saith,
"Go feed my lambs, my wandering sheep, oh, feed!
And all the sinful to my fountain lead."
In the wide brotherhood of man, once made
In God's own image 'neath the Eden shade,
My heart rejoiced; and from my weary eyes
Sleep fled away; and, with a sweet surprise,
I listened to the voice of one who long
Had sung in cadence sweet the gospel song,
And heard him tell, in tones the angels know,
The love of God to sinners here below;
And then, responsive, heard the voices clear
Of some vice-rescued, blood-washed sinners there,
In grateful accents praising God and man,
Who this great work for fallen ones began.
The moments sped; the midnight hour drew nigh,
The midnight stars reached their meridian high:
The moments sped; but still we lingered there,
And holy song, and words of hope and prayer,
Filled the blest hours, till homeward turned our feet,
And, the glad measure of surprise complete,

---

\* Written after visiting the Quincy Home for the Friendless, in Boston, with the chaplain, Rev. Phineas Stowe.

We blessed the home for friendless ones and lone,
And felt that God the enterprise would own, —
Would bless the laborers in their work of love,
And aid their toil with unction from above,
Till the lost spirits of that region find
A shelter in the Friend of all mankind.

## LINES FOR AN AGRICULTURAL FAIR.

FRIENDS, how we all have hailed in grateful
    gladness
  The golden glory of this autumn day!
Hope banished from our hearts the mists of sadness,
  As sunshine rends the cloud-veils all away:
For He who hath the ample harvest given
Still rules with loving justice earth and heaven.

Shall we not trust Him, who, to every sower
  That duly toileth, gives the garner filled?
Shall we not love him, though the silent mower
  Sweeps his relentless scythe, and hearts are chilled?
Love Him and trust Him in the time of sadness,
Oh! just as truly as in hours of gladness!

Yes; for He gives the seed-time and the season
  When hearts, rejoicing, gather ripened grain;
And only hearts rebellious with sin's treason
  Can think of murmuring, when he asks again
For some sweet flower to deck the paths of glory,
For some strong voice to tell the saint's glad story.

So, whether bright or sombre be to-morrow,
   We will be glad and grateful here to-day:
God cannot overwhelm a soul with sorrow,
   That looks with childlike trust to him alway,
And only cares, in sowing or in reaping,
To please the Lord, who giveth smiles for weeping.

The day shall come, when, all our labors ended,
   Each good seed sown, each path of duty trod,
Our faith at last into glad vision blended,
   We shall keep harvest-time at home with God;
And every soul, through Christ, from sin made free,
Shall join the anthem of earth's jubilee.

## THE CROSS AND THE CROWN.

"'TIS heavy, Lord, the cross thou gavest me:
   I scarce can bear it on my weary way."
So sighed a weary pilgrim; but an angel sang,
   "Strength shall be given equal to thy day."

Onward he toiled, that pilgrim worn and sad:
   The cross seemed heavier as he bent him down.
Then angels whispered, "Look up, and be glad;
   For every cross shall change into a crown."

He heard the whisper, so like music sweet;
   His faith the promise grasped; with lifted eye
He saw the green fields for his weary feet,
   Where the still streams of peace flow gently by.

"Forgive my murmur," then the pilgrim cried,
  "And let the cross be heavy if thou wilt:
I'll think of him who once on Calvary died,
  And of the cross he bore for human guilt.

"His was the greatest cross, and his will be
  The brightest crown all future ages through.
O blessed Saviour! make me like to thee,
  Patient and trustful, till thy face I view."

Lo! as he prayed, his cross began to shine
  With lustre like an angel's radiant wing,
And in his soul he felt a peace divine:
  "The cross and crown are one," he then could sing.

'Tis sweet to bear the cross in duty's path;
  'Tis bliss to suffer for the cause of Truth;
To faithful souls is heaven begun on earth,
  And hopeful pilgrims share eternal youth.

## THE QUESTION ANSWERED.*

THE evening hour with soothing quiet came;
  The silver moon rose slowly up the sky;
Crowned with young womanhood, two friends walked forth,
Communing gladly of Life's purpose high.

* Suggested by an incident in the life of Lucy Stone and Antoinette Brown, while fellow-students at Oberlin, Ohio.

The queenly step of one, the taller, ceased:
   She turned, and looked full in her friend's clear eye.
"Can woman reach the pulpit?" then she asked,
   And waited, with a full heart, the reply.

The answer came; but not a hope was born,
   As fell those words upon the querist's heart:
"Woman may labor in full many a field,
   But may not hope to act the preacher's part."

She asked of God,—that woman brave and pure:
   God gave the answer in the wish inspired.
The seed contained the germ; and in God's time
   There came the fruitage which the words desired.

Years passed: and she who answered stood full oft
   Beneath the shelter of our State-House domes;
And legislators heard her soul-full tones,
   Pleading for equal rights in states and homes.

The querist stood in many a pulpit too,
   Proclaiming Christ with hope to bless and save;
Her young heart glad with more than human joy,
   As there she told of bliss beyond the grave.

Both have wrought nobly where few women toil,
   Been pioneers in that cause, pure and high,
Which gives her place to woman by man's side,
   With him to lead immortals to the sky.

Their lives have shown that naught can stay the tide
   Of God's great purpose in its onward flow;
That where man nobly labors for the race,
   There, too, may woman, at God's summons, go.

A quarter-century now hath passed away,
   And many a woman in the pulpit stands,
Ordained to do the pastor's noble work
   By more than laying on of human hands.

O God! we'll trust thee for the days to come,
   Thou who hast guided woman in the Past;
And with a grateful heart thine handmaids sing,
   "The day of righteous freedom dawns at last."

www.ingramcontent.com/pod-product-compliance
Lightning Source LLC
Chambersburg PA
CBHW031250250426
43672CB00029BA/1894